The
Caring
Jesus

The Caring Jesus

A Woman's View
of the
Gospel of John

Helen Kooiman Hosier

HAWTHORN BOOKS, INC.
W. Clement Stone, Publisher
New York

THE CARING JESUS

Library of Congress Catalog Card Number: 74-33587

ISBN: 0-8015-1084-8

1   2   3   4   5   6   7   8   9   10

To
my husband, who
demonstrates the caring
qualities of Jesus

Contents

Preface

A woman in a neighborhood Bible study group startled everyone by stating, "I am tired of a little, skinny, old, emaciated Jesus!"

The Bible presents Jesus as anything but little, skinny, old, or emaciated. John's Gospel, in particular, shows us "the caring Jesus." The Jesus we meet there is a singular man—the personification of perfection, greatness, and love that has never been matched. This man Jesus wrestled with the issues of the world of his day—issues that are not too unlike those of our world; people haven't changed that much nor the things that concern them the most. He contended for things that mattered. Jesus always accepted the challenge of grappling with issues that shaped the destinies of individual lives. Perhaps that is why I see him, especially in John's Gospel, as "the caring Jesus."

He cared deeply. It mattered to him about individuals. They were important. He loved us so much that he came to us. "For God loved the world so much that he gave his only Son so that anyone who believes in him shall not perish but have eternal life" (John 3:16). That is perhaps the most familiar verse in all of the Bible. But what does it really mean? Among other things it tells me that Jesus is the human face of God! That is nothing short of astounding.

This, then, is one woman's eye view of Jesus in the Gospel of John. I see him there as love in action. I send this book forth with the prayer that you will recognize him for all that he is; he cares so very much for you, you know.

Acknowledgments

Scripture quotations identified AV are from the Authorized (King James) Version of the Bible.

Scripture quotations identified NAS are from the *New American Standard Bible*, Copyright 1960, 1962, 1963, 1968, 1971 by The Lockman Foundation, and are used by permission.

Scripture quotations identified PHILLIPS are from *The New Testament in Modern English* (Revised Edition), Copyright 1958 by J. B. Phillips, and are used by permission of the publisher, The Macmillan Company.

Scripture quotations identified *The Amplified Bible* are from *The Amplified Bible*, Copyright 1965 by Zondervan Publishing House, and are used by permission of the publisher.

All other Scripture quotations unidentified are from *The Living Bible Paraphrased*, Copyright © 1971 by Tyndale House Publishers, and are used by permission of the publisher.

All other quotations throughout the book are used by permission of the publishers.

Introduction to the Gospel of John

AUTHORSHIP

No commentator or writer whom I consulted differed in the commonly held view that the author of this Gospel is John, even though he does not identify himself by name. He does refer to himself as "the disciple whom Jesus loved" (see John 13:23; 19:26; 20:2; 21:7, 20, 23–24). No one knew Jesus better than John, yet one senses from his writing that he was a very modest man. John spent the better part of three and a half years in close company with Jesus and the rest of his life as a disciple of the Way.

John's father was Zebedee (21:2), believed to be a fisherman in good circumstances. His mother was Salome (cf. Matt. 27:56; Mark 15:40; John 19:25), a devout follower of the Lord and probably a sister of Jesus' mother, Mary. This would make Jesus and John cousins and may partly explain the close relationship between the two.

DATE AND PLACE OF COMPOSITION

John was probably about twenty-five years of age when Jesus called him (1:35–37). He was the last of the disciples, it is believed, to die and wrote this Gospel long after the other three Gospels had already been written. The latter years of John's life were spent around the city of Ephesus (in Asia Minor). There he taught, preached, and wrote.

The traditional belief is that the Gospel was written not later than the year A.D. 98 and not earlier than the year 80. John had spent some time on the Isle of Patmos, where he had been banished during the reign of Domitian. Later he was allowed to return to the city of Ephesus, where it is generally believed he wrote this not long before his death. There are some who believe, however, that John wrote the Gospel before being exiled to the island.

PURPOSE OF THE GOSPEL

John himself states the purpose for writing this Gospel in the twentieth chapter, the closing sentences: "But these are written, that ye might believe that Jesus is the Christ, the Son of God; and that believing ye might have life through his name."

John undoubtedly wrote this upon the urging of Christian friends. (I can hear them saying, "John, if *anyone* should write an eyewitness account of Jesus' life and teachings, it's you. Please write down some of the things you remember as being most significant.") And I think this is what prompted him. But I am equally certain of the nudging of the Holy Spirit and his guidance and sure leading, because the account is so simple, and yet at the same time so profound as to be unfathomable! It is a paradox that cannot be fully explained.

From careful study you get the feeling that John presupposes that readers have read the other three Gospels (often called the Synoptics). Much of the material found in Matthew, Mark, and Luke is omitted in John's narrative. This does not imply any conflict between John and the Synoptics, but is rather related to John's intended purpose in writing, i.e., an emphasis on the King himself, the Person of Christ, his Deity.

John did not intend to write a complete biography of Christ, but he carefully selects exactly that additional material that was best suited to bring into clear daylight the glory of the Lord, gleaning up what others had passed by in their telling of Jesus' life.

CHARACTERISTICS

This Gospel is rich in contrasts, such as light, darkness; doubt, faith; spirit, flesh; from life to death, earthly, heavenly; love, hate; opposition, fellowship; grief and sadness, joy and gladness; tumult, peace; trouble, trust; to see, to become blind.

Christ's teaching predominates, but not so much in the form of parables (as it is in the Synoptics) but more in elaborate discourses.

This is the Gospel of the seven "I Am's" (6:35; 8:12; 10:9, 11; 11:25; 14:6; and 15:5).

This is also the Gospel that goes into detail regarding what is often called "The Upper Room Discourses" (although there is diversity of opinion as to whether or not chapters thirteen through seventeen *all* took place in the Upper Room).

John speaks of Jesus' miracles as "signs" recorded to fix the reader's attention upon Christ's divine power (the nobleman's son is *healed from a distance* (4:46 ff.); the man at the Pool of Bethesda had been *lying there thirty-eight years* (5:5); the blind man at Jerusalem had been *born blind* (9:1); and Lazarus had already lain in the grave *four days* (11:17).

It now remains for the reader to read for himself and to seek the meaning of the narrative for his own life and experience.

PART I

Manifestation
to the World Begins

1

The Prologue:
This Planet Has Been Visited

The Text: John 1:1–18
The Place: From Everlasting to Everlasting
The Event: John's Introduction of the Person Whom God
Sent to Supply Humanity's Deepest Needs

The word had a Being before the world had a beginning! He that *was* in the beginning, never began, and therefore was *ever without reference to the beginning of time.* He coexisted with the Father: he was eternal.

> In the beginning was the Word,
> and the Word
> was with God, and the Word
> was God.
> The same was
> in the beginning
> with God (John 1:1, 2 AV).

An ancient philosopher said that the first verses of John's Gospel were worthy to be written in letters of gold. In these verses we are introduced to an idiom peculiar to John's writings. John speaks of Christ as "the Word."

It is a magnificent beginning! John gives us no human genealogy regarding Christ. We are carried back into past eternity by the expression "In the beginning," which ante-

3

dates that same expression as found in the first chapter, first verse of the Bible. There we note the beginning of creation— the world and its created beings are *from* the beginning—but the Word was *in* the beginning. There is a difference.

How beautiful it is to know that the Author and Founder of the world is the same Author and Founder of the Word. He was active in the divine counsels from eternity as a co-ordinate agent, coexistent as a distinct Personality.

As John surveys the stream of history from the beginning to the moment of his writing, he gloriously proclaims:

> All things were made by him;
> and without him
> was not any thing made
> that was made (vs. 3 AV)

THE VEILED UNVEILING

It is characteristic of light to shine forth. Light is self-evidencing. It makes itself known. God is the original of life and light, and the manifestation of himself through the Son is evidence of the Father's desire to impart that eternal life into those who will believe in and accept this glorious Light.

John's sentences are described as joining together like overlapping shingles. The structure is beautiful.

> In him was life;
> and the life was the light of men.
> And the light shineth in darkness;
> and the darkness
> comprehended it not (vss. 4, 5 AV).

Light was focused in a Person. This was Love operating, and all things of earth, especially human life, were to know the light of God's love in a new and radiant revelation.

The very light seen in nature is evidence of the existence of a power far greater than anything the human mind can explain or comprehend. He who commanded the light that is in the world to shine out of darkness was himself the Light shining in darkness.

It is because men have turned away from this Light and followed the vain imaginings of their minds and hearts, preferring the darkness to the Light, that their own dark, evil ways have eclipsed the way so that they cannot see it. It was, therefore, wholly necessary for God to send that Light *into* the world in a bodily Form to dispel the darkness. And so he came, John says, as "the true Light to shine on everyone coming into the world" (vs. 9).

> He was in the world,
>   and the world
>   was made by him,
>   and the world
>   knew him not (vs. 10 AV).

Tragedy of tragedies! He made the world and the world didn't even recognize him when he came!

> He came unto his own
>   and his own
>   recognized him not (vs. 11 AV).

Even in his own land and among his own people, the Jews, to whom he first came, he was not accepted. And it all happened in the fullness of time—according to God's own timetable—immortal God himself lifted the veil from all eternity (so that now more than ever men would be without excuse) and sent his greatest communication to the world in the Person of his Son.

That Christ was actually in the world is an awesome thought. That the Holy God who created the universe actually came to cohabit this sinful, polluted world can scarcely be fathomed. He left a world of bliss and glory to live here in this melancholy, miserable mound of dirt called Earth. Human history would never be the same again!

FAITH ISSUES IN LIFE

Christ's purpose in coming was to bring reconciliation between children of the world and their Father from whom they were estranged. Certainly no greater honor has ever come upon this planet than that it was visited by none other than God in the Person of his Son.

The great drama of the unfolding of faith that issues in life is now set forth. John shows how we can become true "children of God," and it has nothing to do with heredity or environment. It is strictly a gift, and it is so easy to receive.

> But to all who received him, he gave the right to become children of God. (vs. 12 AV).

One of the tragic minor chords in the New Testament is found here in John's Gospel, and it is a dissonant chord that is being perpetuated yet today: He was in the world, and the world was made by him, and the world knew him not. God in Christ became our Contemporary so that by becoming one of us we might become more like him.

Those who lived in Jesus' time, John tells us, "beheld his glory—the glory of the only Son of the heavenly Father." But although others of us have not seen that glorious Light in his actual human form, still we too can say that we have seen his glory as it sheds its Light and radiance upon us from the written Word and creation.

Jesus' principal activity while here upon earth was to teach and patiently convey "grace and truth" (vs. 14). Those who recognized him had their lives transformed. But that is still exactly what happens today, for God's plan was not fulfilled by simply bringing some of Jesus' contemporaries into the family of God. For all those who could not come into contact with Jesus it was necessary that his life and purpose in coming be preserved. The Gospel is for *all* men everywhere. Thus we begin to see the purpose of John's Gospel already spelled out in these first verses in chapter one.

For the law was given by Moses, but grace and truth came
by Jesus Christ (vs. 17 AV).

The prologue reaches its climax when it mentions, for the
first time, the historic title "Jesus Christ" and asserts his
unique Personality as being "the only begotten Son from the
Father."

We are separated by over nineteen hundred years from
Jesus' human pilgrimage, but in this Gospel we still see the
supreme evidence for his divinity in his grace and truth.

Martin Luther said of this Gospel: "Never in my life have
I read a book written in simpler words than this, and yet the
words are inexpressible." I find myself in agreement. I came
away from the first eighteen verses of this narration with the
vivid impression that God cared so much for you and me that
he decided to enter the mainstream of human history in order
to do something about its wretched condition. He was and is
the caring Jesus.

2

The Herald:
Meet the Forerunner of Christ

The Text: John 1:18–34
The Place: Bethany, a Village on the Other Side of the Jordan River
The Event: John's Witness to Christ as Being the Son of God (With Background Information on John the Baptist's Life)

How was God going to reveal Jesus' identity so that men would recognize this divine Light that was in their midst? How were men to come to the conclusion that Jesus was God incarnate?

The apostle John, in understated magnificence, ushers in the one who had the tremendous privilege of introducing Christ to the world.

We must not confuse John the Baptist with the apostle John (who wrote this Gospel). John the Baptist and Jesus were drawn together by twin ties. First, both of their births were announced by the angel Gabriel. Second, John and Jesus were cousins—John's mother, Elisabeth, and Jesus' mother, Mary, were first cousins.

John was a distinguished blessing to earth. It is one thing to be considered great in the world's eyes, but quite another thing to have it said of you that you are "great in the sight of the Lord," and this is what the angel said John would be.

At the time of John's circumcision, Zechariah spoke these prophetic words: "And you, child, will be called the prophet of the Most High; for you will go before the Lord to prepare his ways. . . ." (Luke 1:76).

John was a tough man, weathered, undoubtedly, by years of solitude living in the desert. His appearance caused people to sit up and take notice, and his tongue struck like lightning. He used words like hammers to pound men's hearts into submission, to switch their loyalties, and to ready them for God's invasion. This was his calling, and he would be true to it.

So it was that John was not speaking for himself, but he was the voice of God to those who swarmed to hear him. People poured out of the cities and villages to hear this Goliath of a man who minced no words. Understandably, John the Baptist was hated by many, feared by others, and honored by some. So effective was he that people wondered if he was the promised Messiah. Without doubt, John was being discussed everywhere. But John quickly put an end to people's wondering, declaring and denying flatly, "I am not the Christ" (see John 1:19–22).

How important it is that we get the picture, for it is this man whom God chose to set the stage for the arrival of Christ. And how effective he was! He made an impact as he faithfully bore witness to the Light. Generally speaking, Light witnesses to itself, but to those who shut their eyes against the Light it is necessary that there should be those who bear witness to it. Matthew Henry has stated that Christ's Light needs not man's testimony, but the world's darkness does!

John the Baptist was himself a light (as we all are when we are living for Christ), but he enlightened only Jerusalem and Judea, and the region around about the Jordan where he baptized.

When questioned as to his identity, John gave as his only credentials the fact that he was "a voice crying in the wilderness, 'Prepare ye the way of the Lord.'" Ironside remarks: "You cannot see a voice, you can only hear it. John did not want them [those questioning him] to become occupied with him. It was his delight simply to exalt the One whose herald he was, and in this John becomes the example for every servant of God. . . . He was not concerned about himself if only Christ could be glorified." [1]

THE GREAT PRONOUNCEMENT

The next day John saw Jesus coming toward him and said, "Look! There is the Lamb of God who takes away the world's sin! He is the one I was talking about when I said, 'Soon a man far greater than I is coming, who existed long before me!' I didn't know he was the one, but I am here baptizing with water in order to point him out to the nation of Israel" (vss. 29–31).

This utterance of John has to be acknowledged as one of the greatest truths of the Gospel. John used imagery that was familiar to the people. All through the centuries Israel had known of the sacrificial lamb. Isaiah 53 speaks prophetically of the Lamb of God who would be wounded for our transgressions and bruised for our iniquities.

John held a very unique place in relation to Christ, but there has never been a humbler, less exalted servant of God than John the Baptist. No wonder Jesus said of him that of those born of women there was not one greater than John.

In answer to the question they might ask as to how he, John, really knew that this was the long-expected Messiah, John says,

"I have beheld the Spirit descending as a dove out of heaven; and He remained upon Him.
"And I did not recognize Him, but He who sent me to baptize in water said to me, 'He upon whom you see the Spirit descending and remaining upon Him, this is the one who baptizes in the Holy Spirit,'
"And I have seen, and have borne witness that this is the Son of God" (vss. 32–34 NAS).

[1] H. A. Ironside, *Gospel of John* (New York: Loizeaux Bros., Inc., n.d.), p. 22.

As the people looked upon this shaggy Bedouin preacher who had burst upon the scene with such thundering and powerful words, it must have made quite an impression.

John's eloquent testimony reaches its climax in the glorious words: "He is the Son of God." John's testimony was the echo of the voice that spoke to him from heaven at the time of Jesus' baptism. It is an echo that never fades so long as we take up the refrain. John the Baptist was the first of many succeeding heralds. I trust that includes you, the reader.

3

The First Disciples:
The Dawning of a New Day

The Text: John 1:35–51
The Place: Bethany Beyond the Jordan; and in Galilee
The Event: Jesus Starting on the Pathway of his Public
Ministry and the Gathering of the First
Disciples

God has various methods of drawing people to himself. When Jesus gave the first invitation to men to follow him, it was gentle, soft-spoken: "Follow me." And they did—John, Andrew, Peter, Philip, Nathanael—the nucleus of the Church in its very beginning. The narrative of the call of the first disciples shows clearly the birth of faith. That is always the dawning of a great new day for anyone who dares to step out and follow Jesus.

How Was Faith Awakened in Jesus'
First Followers?

How does one explain the birth of faith? Faith is always awakened in the hearts of believers in response to *testimony* concerning who Christ is. John was but the first of a long succession of believers willing to cry out and take a firm stand for Jesus. According to biblical evidence, therefore, it can be said that the first form of testimony that secured followers for

Christ was that of John the Baptist. How much the world needs men and women like that.

A DAY OF INDELIBLE IMPRESSIONS

After John the Baptist declared Jesus to be the Son of God, we read:

> The following day as John was standing with two of his disciples, Jesus walked by. John looked at him intently and then declared, "See! There is the Lamb of God!" (John 1:35, 36).

On the previous day John had pointed Jesus out as the Sin-Bearer (see vs. 29) and the Spirit-Baptizer (see vs. 33). Now once again John identifies Jesus as the "Lamb of God." Take heart, those of you who have pointed Jesus out to unbelieving friends and relatives and get no immediate response. It was not the first proclamation of John the Baptist that secured for Jesus his first followers, but the second.

> Then John's two disciples turned and followed Jesus. Jesus looked around and saw them following. "What do you want?" he asked them (vss. 37, 38).

Jesus had his back to these disciples, but he was aware of them and their following after him. What comfort there is in that thought—Christ always takes immediate cognizance of the first movements of any individual toward him.

REQUEST FOR AN AUDIENCE

The first words to fall from Jesus' lips as he began his public ministry are worth examining. What he said was put in the form of a question. And what a question it is! It plumbs the very depths of life. "What are you seeking? What do you want?" It is a question we all need to ask ourselves. Only insofar as we are willing to answer honestly can we hope to find meaning in life.

Jesus did not reprimand these two men for their boldness in intruding into his company; on the contrary, his words opened the door for conversation with him.

And they said to Him, "Rabbi (which translated means Teacher), where are You staying?" (vs. 38b NAS).

They did want something from Jesus, though precisely what may have been unclear in their thinking. This Man Jesus had such magnetism, such charisma, that they knew they wanted to know more about him and more from him, and they were willing to drop everything just to follow him.

If they had wanted to be conventionally religious, they could have joined the Pharisees; if they had wanted money, they could have gotten that by becoming tax collectors or better fishermen, or by pursuing some profitable trade of their day; if they had had political aspirations, they could have gone to work in Herod's court; if they had been anxious to overthrow the Romans, they had the option of joining the Zealots who were plotting against the occupation army. But there was much more than mere curiosity involved in the decision of Andrew and John that day that caused them, in answer to his question, to inquire where he lived.

They wanted more than a five or ten minute conversation with Jesus on a dusty road. The impression comes across that they were anxious to have time with him. The fact that they address him as Rabbi intimates that they recognized him as being a *master*, a teaching master. The Jews reserved that title for their doctors and learned men only. The word *rabbi* in its original connotation means *a great man*, one who has *much in him*. How right they were in giving him that honored title. Never has there been such a *Rabbi* as Jesus, such a *great one*. The Bible declares that in him were *hid all the treasures of wisdom and knowledge*.

There was no delay, immediately the disciples went to the place where he was staying. Make no mistake in your think-

ing; if you will take but one step even in the direction of
seeking to learn more about Christ, you will be drawn into the
circle of his care.

When once you have seen God in Jesus, then you are
certain of God forever. Unquestionably, that is what happened
to Andrew and John. Their hearts were won by Jesus, and
the result was immediately evident. Notice their next actions:

> Andrew then went to find his brother Peter and told
> him, "We have found the Messiah!" And he brought Peter
> to meet Jesus (vss. 41, 42a).

A CHAIN REACTION SETS IN

Having come in vital contact with the long-looked-for
Messiah, Andrew's immediate concern was for his brother
Peter. Here is another form of testimony that secures followers for Christ. Personal witness to relatives is often the
most difficult of all; but can be the most effective. Think of
the great loss that would have incurred to the cause of Christ
if Andrew had not brought Peter to where Jesus was! What a
dynamic power Peter became as leader of the Church in its
infancy!

Now, because of the faithful testimony of his brother, Peter
stands in the Presence of Christ. Can you see Andrew in his
excitement and great newfound joy grabbing his big brother
Peter by the shoulders and saying, "Come with me, John and
I have found the Messiah!"

Andrew didn't waste any time. What he had seen in Christ
was so good he couldn't wait to share it with his brother he
loved, so that he, too, could see for himself. Such love is a
prerequisite for every true follower of Jesus. Think it not
strange, you who are reading this, if someone dear to you in
the intimacy of your family circle pleads with you to look
into the Bible where you can meet Jesus, or if they invite you
to listen to their testimony of what Jesus has done in their life,
or to hear the testimony of someone else. They are only following the biblical pattern. Can you find it in your heart to

understand the motive that prompts someone to speak to you of Christ? It is because that someone cares for you, even as Jesus does.

Andrew spoke humbly, he showed excitement and joy, and he also spoke intelligently. Here is a pattern for those of us who want to be used in introducing others to Christ. Andrew did not seek to introduce Peter to a new creed or doctrine; he was not going to ask him to become a member of some organization or to engage in a series of complicated ceremonial observances. His only concern was that Peter meet the Messiah. The effect of Andrew's being with Christ was observable by Peter. What a witness this is to the testimony of Andrew!

John, too, thought of his brother, James, who also becomes a disciple.

CALLED BY CHRIST

There is still another way by which individuals are called to become followers of Christ. This, for some, is the most difficult to understand, we might even say the most mysterious. The Holy Spirit is that unseen Power that though not discernible with the human eye is nonetheless real and active.

The day following Jesus' time with Andrew and John, and the bringing of Peter to Jesus, we see Jesus venturing forth to Galilee (vs. 43a). He takes a hand in the business of finding men.

He found Philip and told him, "Come with me" (vs. 43b).

Philip was found by Christ! What encouragement that is. The power of Christ knows no boundaries; it will reach out and find all those who are to belong to him.

Perhaps someone is reading this who has felt a strange but strong tug at his heart. No one has invited you to follow Christ, but curiosity compelled you to purchase this book that implies by its title that somewhere "out there" there is a caring Jesus. Or perhaps someone gave this book to you. Whatever or however, you now have it in your possession. What Jesus did for Philip, he desires to do for you.

Philip became a disciple in response to a direct call from Christ. While he had a confrontation with the actual Person of Christ—he could see him, he could reach out and touch him —that same Christ is alive today, and through his Holy Spirit he is extending the invitation to you. "Follow me," is his appeal.

PHILIP'S CONVICTION AND SUBSEQUENT ACTION

Philip lost no time in finding another follower, Nathanael, and told him,

> "We have found the Messiah!—the very person Moses and the prophets told about! His name is Jesus, the son of Joseph from Nazareth!" (vs. 45).

Philip's joy and enthusiasm spilled out as he testified with deep conviction. It was to his advantage that he was so well acquainted with the Scriptures of the Old Testament. His mind was prepared to receive the Light of the world when he came into view. But Nathanael did not lightly assent to what Philip said. He raised the question,

> "Nazareth!" exclaimed Nathanael. "Can anything good come from there?" (vs. 46).

Towns have a way of acquiring a reputation. Bethsaida, the city of Andrew, Peter, and Philip, was considered a wicked place; yet even there was a remnant of good.

Bethsaida had its reputation and so did Nazareth. Nathanael was a man of sincerity; his objection arose from ignorance and som prejudice. Surely there is a lesson here for us: Often we make foolish and ill-natured observations colored by things that have happened in the past and by limited knowledge; our mistaken prejudices color the thinking of others. We need to make certain we know all the facts whereof we speak.

There was something else that influenced Nathanael's reaction. More than likely Nathanael knew that the predicted
birthplace of the Messiah was Bethlehem, not Nazareth.
Philip blundered in calling Jesus the son of Joseph from
Nazareth. Observation: young beginners in matters of religion
are subject to mistakes. Philip was no exception.

This difficulty did not give rise to doubtful disputation.
Nathanael was not unreasonable and it did not cause inaction;
instead, he comes to Christ, to see for himself.

Philip displayed wisdom. He didn't know enough to give a
satisfactory answer to Nathanael. That is not unusual for
babes in the faith. We may know enough to satisfy ourselves
and yet not be able to say enough to silence the objections of
others. And so Philip simply says,

> "Just come and see for yourself" (vs. 46b).

That is the answer we must give to those who raise doubts
concerning Christ.

To those who have doubts I would point to Philip and his
friend. Philip was able to turn Nathanael in the direction of
faith by a few short words. That avenue of faith is open to all
who, with open mind, are willing to find out for themselves
who Christ is. What happened to Nathanael was startling indeed!

> As they approached, Jesus said, "Here comes an honest
> man—a true son of Israel." "How do you know what I
> am like?" Nathanael demanded. And Jesus replied, "I could
> see you under the fig tree before Philip found you."
> Nathanael replied, "Sir, you are the Son of God—the
> King of Israel!" Jesus asked him, "Do you believe all this
> just because I told you I had seen you under the fig tree?
> You will see greater proofs than this. You will even see
> heaven open and the angels of God coming back and forth
> to me, the Messiah" (vss. 47–51).

What a marvelous manifestation of himself this was! And
Nathanael, quite frankly, was impressed. In fact, he was more

than impressed, he was convinced! His coming to Jesus was not in vain.

It is the prerogative infallibly of God to know *all* persons and all things (cf. Isa. 11:2–5). Like a flash of brilliant light, I think, Nathanael saw that day who Christ was, and what power resided in him.

What a compliment Jesus paid to Nathanael: I know you to be a sincere follower of the good example of Israel, you are genuine, honest, without guile! Oh, to be able to have that said of us by Christ. I can't know what is in your heart by looking at your face, any more than you can know me that way; but Christ can. All things are naked and open before him. "The Lord knows those who are really his" (2 Tim. 2:19a).

The response of Nathanael was a noble acknowledgment that his prejudices concerning Christ had vanished. With modesty befitting his true nature, he freely confesses, "Rabbi, You are the Son of God; You are the King of Israel" (vs. 49 NAS).

The tenderness with which Christ deals with Nathanael strikes a responsive chord. He promises him greater help for the confirmation and increase of his faith in the future.

Each of Jesus' disciples, in their initial encounter with him, recognized him in a unique way. It showed in their response as they left all to follow him. In the poem entitled *Following Christ* the poet describes what happens when someone heeds Christ's call:

> Does Christ save you from your sin?
>   Call Him Savior!
> Does He free you from the slavery of your passions?
>   Call Him Redeemer!
> Does He teach you as no one else has taught you?
>   Call Him Teacher!
> Does He mould and master your life?
>   Call Him Master!
> Does He shine upon the pathway that is dark to you?
>   Call Him Guide!

Does He reveal God to you?
    Call Him the Son of God!
Does He reveal man?
    Call Him the Son of Man!
Or, in following Him, are your lips silent in your capacity
    to define Him, and His influence upon you?
    Call Him by no name, but follow Him!
                  (Howard S. Bliss—source unknown)

HE CALLS BECAUSE HE CARES

As we look at these first followers of Christ, it is well to remind ourselves that from the standpoint of earthly position, not one of these men could lay claim to anything of special importance or of any great note. They were not men of outstanding achievement. They had no claim to fame. These first men, pioneers actually out on the trail following in the footsteps of Jesus, were so very ordinary. What encouragement that gives to those of us who are likewise so unimpressively ordinary. I am sure God must think quite a lot of ordinary people, he made so many of us!

I shall never cease to be amazed that God should choose to use us to communicate for him. God chose different men, different personalities, different methods. Is there one best method to use to lead men to Christ? Humanity is infinite in variety; note Jesus at work. God has many ways of drawing men to himself. Let us make certain we do not stereotype our methods but allow the Holy Spirit freedom to work in and through us. Neither let us lay such great emphasis upon organization. Jesus simply moved in upon the scene, calling out an Andrew, the cautious one; John, the poet, the dreamer, the mystic, the seer; Simon, simple yet powerful, with all the essentials of basic humanity so strong in his personality, but yet just as weak as weak can be; Philip, shy, but a man who had friends; and Nathanael, the guileless, no deceit, transparent and open.

The Christian is not one who has gone all the way with Christ (none of us has), but the Christian is one who has

found the right road, says writer Charles L. Allen. Those first
followers of Christ found the right road that day so long ago.
The poet has written:

> Whenever I come on kelp-stained nets
> Drying along the sands,
> I think of four bronzed fishermen,
> And my heart understands
> How joyfully they laid aside
> Their nets by Galilee
> To follow one clear Beacon Light
> Across eternity.
> (Leslie Savage Clark—source unknown)

The great hunger of the world today is for Jesus. The world
may not recognize this as their greatest need, but it is true.
Our local newspaper carried a People Quiz and asked the
question: What do most people really want out of life? The
answer stated that as people mature into adulthood, the things
they want most become less and less materialistic and focus
more on happiness and satisfaction, appearance and personality, love, family relationships, health, and success in
vocation. Top priority included the wish to achieve a happy
life, to enjoy good health, to be successful in one's calling—
and also prominently mentioned was a *fervent wish for world
peace*.[1]

The Bible says of Jesus that he is our way of peace (Eph.
2:14). As we proceed with the study in John's Gospel, we
shall see that Jesus' legacy to his followers was this very thing
—*peace*. It comes only through Jesus. He alone is the hope of
of the world. The healing of the world is in Jesus. If you
would find durable satisfaction in life, if you want meaning,
purpose, and all the things mentioned in this cross-section
interview of people from across the country, then you must,
like Jesus' first followers, respond to his call of "Follow me."
Believe him, believe the record, there is no other way. He
calls because he cares.

[1] *Family Weekly* (magazine section of *The Salinas Californian*), Novem-
ber 24, 1974, p. 16.

4

The Beginning of His Signs:
The Miraculous Can Happen

The Text: John 2:1–11
The Place: Cana in Galilee
The Event: A Wedding; Jesus Performs His First Miracle

Jesus loved people, loved to be with them, loved them for their own sakes, and found joy in associating with them. We see him in the Gospel accounts regularly attending feasts. He enjoyed them. Love, joy, and brotherliness were there, and the essence of hospitality. He approved of this. He was not a hermit or fanatic. In John chapter two we have a scene that illustrates Jesus' perfect humanity as we see him, his mother, and his disciples at a wedding in Cana in Galilee (John 2:1, 2).

It is difficult to understand how, by looking at the life of Jesus, one can possibly think that by becoming a Christian and accepting Christ into one's life you are robbed of joy and gladness. On the contrary, by his presence at this wedding and his part in the feast we have a demonstration of the claim he made that he came so we might "have life, and have it more abundantly."

If you have the erroneous idea that sourness is a sign of sainthood, or gloom is a condition of godliness, then lay those thoughts to rest once and for all. This is simply not true. If you know any joyless, so-called "saints," then I would question whether they really understand the caring Jesus.

An observation and a plea to Christians reading this: A cheerful, happy disposition is a great recommendation to others that in Christ you have found someone who imparts joy and happiness to your life. We are to be walking visuals showing to others the transforming power of Jesus. By walking with him we are not deprived of anything; on the contrary, the added dimension will give new radiance, sparkle, and zest.

Although Jesus was God's Son who entered the mainstream of human history in the Person of Mary's Baby, Jesus, he was also uniquely Mary's Son. The relationship between Mother and Son was the closest possible human relationship. He did not make her feel unnatural. God had requested of Mary that her life be used for a special, holy purpose, and she gave of herself willingly. Jesus would not have us feel unnatural in our relationship with him either.

Marriages were celebrated with festivals in token of joy and friendly respect, and for the confirming of love. Jesus' attendance at this wedding shows the Lord's approval of that intimate relationship of holy marriage.

A Problem at the Wedding Feast

At the wedding a most embarrassing thing happened to the host:

> The wine supply ran out during the festivities, and Jesus'
> mother came to him with the problem (vs. 3).

Hospitality is the supreme obligation in Eastern culture and the situation at this wedding was serious. Of course the host was distressed and shared the problem with Mary. She was a resourceful woman, but this presented a bigger problem than she was capable of handling. She acquaints Jesus with the difficulty. The naturalness of her approach to him arrests our attention. There is no hesitation, but rather a direct openness,

"They have no more wine" (vs. 3 PHILLIPS).

In Mary's act we see that we, too, can address ourselves to Christ, spreading out our needs and the needs of others before him, and then refer ourselves to him to do as he pleases. Actually, Jesus' mother didn't request him to do anything about the problem, but one senses that she expected him to do something.

Jesus' reply to Mary has long been the subject of much conjecture.

> "Woman, what have I to do with thee? Mine hour is not yet come" (vs. 4 AV).

Some think the Lord spoke a bit roughly, but we may be sure he would not have embarrassed or hurt his mother in any way. Whatever he said, whatever he actually meant, it was said in love. He was about to step out of the intimacy of the family circle into that ministry for which he came into the world, and he knew it. Jesus didn't tell Mary that he wouldn't work a miracle, but one senses that he wanted her to know that she must not expect miracles or mighty signs from him just to please his relatives or friends. Jesus worked miracles in accordance with God's counsel. What he did from this time on he did as the Son of God.

The word *woman* as used here by Jesus is meant to convey intense tenderness. The same word was on the lips of Jesus when he hung on the cross and spoke his last words to his mother, affectionately commending her to John's care.

As a woman, I identify most closely with G. Campbell Morgan's explanation. To the longing of the mother-heart of Mary, Jesus was in effect saying, "Mother, mine, I know what you want, but you do not understand; there are limitations to your understanding of me. Mother of my flesh, dear to my heart, Mother under whose heart my life was enshrined when God prepared for me my body; you have been watching over me all these years, and now that I seem to be moving out into public work, you are anxious I shall do something that will reveal the meaning of my personality and mission, but my hour is not yet come." [1]

In succeeding chapters we shall see Jesus alluding to "that hour." Throughout his earthly life, knowing why he was sent by the Father, Jesus had before him "that hour." Jesus' first reference to "that hour" was made to his mother, and the last to his Father (John 17:1).

By accepting Jesus' gentle reproof as she did, Mary showed that she was satisfied with his reply. The situation would be taken care of immediately; and I think, too, that she understood better her new role as being subservient to Christ. To the servants she simply said,

"Do whatever he tells you to" (vs. 5).

She spoke those words with a greater depth of meaning and more confidence than appears on the surface. They reveal unbounded faith in Jesus. Mary neither disputed with Christ about what he said nor did she question him. Her meekness is exemplary. There is much by the way of practical application here for us. Whatever Christ says, let *us* obey and do. Mary's comment to the servants is evidence of the fact that she encouraged herself with hope that Jesus would do what was best. Does the fact that Jesus cares about your dilemma seem a reality to you?

THE BEGINNING OF HIS SIGNS

With quiet dignity, Jesus put forth his creative power by turning water into wine (vss. 6–10). The miracle was accomplished! He produced immediate results that were normally obtained only through slower processes. The fact that "the ruler of the feast" testified to the excellence of the wine constitutes an unprejudiced witness to the perfection of Christ's work.

In John's Gospel all the miracles are events that reveal the

---

[1] G. Campbell Morgan, *The Gospel According to John* (Old Tappan, N.J., Fleming H. Revell Co., n.d.), p. 48.

mind and heart of Jesus and, through him, the mind and heart of God. Remember this as you come across Jesus performing miracles, or signs, from here on in this Gospel. These miracles, therefore, are the revelation of two things: *power* and *pity*. These are signs that Jesus cares. In the actualities of human life, we have a caring Jesus.

> This miracle at Cana in Galilee was Jesus' first public demonstration of his heaven-sent power. And his disciples believed that he really was the Messiah (vs. 11).

Jesus himself is the greatest miracle of all time. The response of Jesus' first followers is the response he is still seeking today. Can your belief in Jesus be established as a result of observing the power and work of this one who cares so much for you?

If we are to experience divine action on our behalf, if there is to be lasting change in our lives, then we must be willing to share our needs with him. We must make our requests known and then let God take care of them in his own way. The miraculous can happen to you.

5

Voice of Authority:
Love With a Whip?

The Text: John 2:13–25
The Place: Jerusalem in the Temple Area
The Event: The Jewish Passover Celebration; Jesus' First
Purging of the Temple

I protest any weak ideas or arguments that would portray Jesus as effeminate, somehow lacking in strength or the ability to exert power and show authority. There are those who would play down the events as described in the last half of John 2. Somehow they feel this is out of character with the gracious, loving image of Jesus that is usually presented. But there it is, in black and white; boldly it confronts us:

> Then it was time for the annual Jewish Passover celebration, and Jesus went to Jerusalem.
> In the Temple area he saw merchants selling cattle, sheep, and doves for sacrifices, and money changers behind their counters. Jesus made a whip from some ropes and chased them all out, and drove out the sheep and oxen, scattering the money changers' coins over the floor and turning over their tables! Then going over to the men selling doves, he told them, "Get these things out of here. Don't turn my Father's House into a market!" (John 2:11–16).

Jesus angry? Indeed! Righteous indignation spilling over. To many this is the most astonishing event in Jesus' life. His emotions were strong, but always under control. Were they out of control then? Here we see Jesus as he embodies the very fury of God; yet, this is also Love in action.

This was Jesus' first recorded visit to Jerusalem as Messiah. Christ kept the Passover because, being made under the law, he would teach by his example obedience to divine institutions. Wasn't Jesus interested in winning the Jewish religious leaders over? Surely he knew what this action would do to his standing in their eyes! Why alienate them this way by lashing out so strongly? Couldn't he have accomplished the same results in some less demonstrative way? Most sins aroused in Jesus nothing but pity; not so this time as he deals with these religious leaders.

In the Old Testament book of Malachi we read: "And the Lord, whom ye seek, shall suddenly come to his temple, even the messenger of the covenant, whom ye delight in: behold, he shall come, saith the Lord of hosts" (Mal. 3:1).

> Then his disciples remembered this prophecy from the Scriptures: "Concern for God's House will be my undoing" (vs. 17).

Historians say that sometimes the pilgrims coming to Jerusalem for this feast numbered two to three million. Everyone was required to pay the required shekel. And then there was the selling of the animals in the outer Temple court. Sacrificial animals were brought in and sold in the thousands. They had to be officially passed as perfect, and no one could do this but the Temple officials. The monopoly was extreme. There were the tables of the money changers piled high with every sort of foreign money, which had to be changed into Temple currency. It was a place of dust and noise and confusion.

And where did the profits go? To the priests, of course. They were enormously wealthy. The abuse was obvious to Jesus. Disorder, greed, dishonesty and extortion are entirely out of order anywhere, but even more out of place in the

Temple and its courts. Can you see him in fierce indignation striding through their midst, asserting himself as Lord of the Temple? Forcibly he expelled them. We sense his displeasure with anyone who would make religion a matter of personal gain.

Of course, Christ was in control of himself and the situation. He knew exactly what he was doing; he knew the action would result unquestionably in definite hostility toward him by the priestly hierarchy. It was an act of holiness designed to teach the people that their greatest need was for spiritual cleansing, and that merely going through the motions in so-called acts of worship and sacrificing was not enough. There isn't enough money in all the world, or enough sacrificial offerings that a person can make to purchase God's favor.

NEW LIGHT THROWN ON OLD TESTAMENT SCRIPTURE

The Jewish leaders were indignant! Hostile! They demanded that Jesus vindicate this drastic action (vss. 18–22).

But there was something in Jesus' manner, as well as his words, that awed the onlookers. Jesus had the manner of a prophet, and they did not resist the authority by which he spoke and acted.

Earthly fathers are never perfect; but a good father takes care of his children, is devoted to them, and loves them. A good father will even get angry when something happens that affects his children adversely. And good fathers have been known to act with whips in their hands! Love with a whip is still love!

In this chapter we have seen an angry Jesus. An anemic Christ would not have done for the world what Jesus, in righteous anger, did that day. Let us not cancel out this event in the life of our Lord; let's not make excuses for it as if he did something that was out of character. When we do that, we cancel Christianity as a vital and living force. Through it all I trust you have seen Love pulsating, acting on your behalf.

6

The Gospel of the New Birth:
Born Again?

The Text: John 3
The Place: Jerusalem
The Event: Jesus' Private Conference with Nicodemus

Come to Jesus at night if you wish; he keeps evening hours; in fact, no appointment is necessary. Jesus is available to the inquiring mind and hungry heart at any hour, day or night. Come to Jesus alone if you prefer, away from the wondering gaze of others. Jesus is easy of access; he won't make you feel ill at ease, nor will he leave you in your aloneness. In his presence you will feel surrounded by love and understanding. You will discover for yourself what a man named Nicodemus learned the night he ventured forth.

> After dark one night a Jewish religious leader named Nicodemus, a member of the sect of the Pharisees, came for an interview with Jesus (John 3:1).

I'm so glad Nicodemus came. Contrary to what many say who regard his seeking a nighttime tryst with Jesus as the act of a coward, I say all praise to this one who dared to put legs on his wonderings as he sought answers to the questions in his mind and the conflict in his heart. Whatever you do, come. The time of day and manner in which you approach Christ is irrelevent. Alone or accompanied, you are assured of an audience with someone who cares and has respect for your personality.

Nicodemus was definitely what could be called the man at the top. He was from the upper stratum of society, with all the culture and religious training of a typical Jewish rabbi. He was a Pharisee, and conspicuous among them for his learning and ability. He was even a member of the Sanhedrin, that council of seventy members who ruled the political as well as the religious life of the nation. But having said that, let me hasten to add that he was courteous, modest, respectful to Jesus and even friendly. His position made any contact with Jesus hazardous. After all, when you are in the public eye and individual thinking is influenced by popular opinion, you must be careful.

Let us not miss the significance of Nicodemus' opening remark to Jesus and the term by which he addresses Jesus, calling him "Rabbi." Here was this great figure in the scholarly and religious world of his day recognizing with all cordiality this one who was not being looked upon so kindly by his contemporaries.

> "Rabbi," Nicodemus said, "we know that thou art a teacher come from God; for no man can do these miracles that thou doest except God be with him" (vs. 2 AV).

Nicodemus, it appears, had been a silent listener to the words of Jesus and an interested observer of Jesus' miracles. Nicodemus was an honest seeker after truth. But his courteous introductory remark was unsatisfactory to Jesus. Why? Because Nicodemus had noted Jesus' signs, the miracles, and this was not enough. Jesus regretted attention given to miracles only.

There are a lot of Nicodemus-like people in the world today. They reverence spiritual things and may even attend church with some degree of regularity—but it's not enough. Notice Jesus' direct response as he cuts through externals to get to the heart of the matter. Jesus interrupted Nicodemus' nice words:

> "With all the earnestness I possess I tell you this: Unless you are born again, you can never get into the Kingdom of God" (vs. 3).

THE SHOCK TREATMENT

Observe Jesus, the Great Physician, as he tells the man who is up and out that he not only needs heart surgery, but he must first of all be born again. Jesus gave Nicodemus a sort of shock treatment as he brushed aside Nicodemus' initial comment. Jesus' abruptness was no accident. He cared about this man. Jesus had a remarkable pupil on his hands; but Nicodemus had a remarkable Teacher. Reputation and position were irrelevent to Jesus; the state of a man's soul—the inner man—was what really mattered.

Jesus saw what was going on in Nicodemus' heart, and he would enter that closed door. He came to seek and to save the lost, and this learned Pharisee, even with all his religious knowledge, was just as lost as the vilest, most down and out sinner. Oftentimes those who think they know the Scriptures best are the most difficult to reach. Jesus *had* to penetrate Nicodemus' thinking, he *had* to jar loose Nicodemus' outer defenses, he *had* to jolt him so that he would consider Jesus' message. Nevertheless, it is somewhat frightening to hear Jesus telling such a man as this that until he is born again he cannot see the Kingdom of God. Knowledge of the Scriptures alone will not suffice; Jesus said it, not I, "You *must be* born again."

Into the great and magnificent mind of Nicodemus Jesus poured the deepest and most difficult lesson that he had to give—the fact of being born again. Nicodemus no doubt had been the recipient of many honors bestowed upon him in his lifetime, but no greater honor would ever come his way than that Jesus chose him as the one into whom this wonderful teaching regarding the need for rebirth was poured. Nicodemus faltered, his mind in the delivery room, as Jesus used a physical illustration to show spiritual truth.

"Born again!" exclaimed Nicodemus. "What do you mean? How can an old man go back into his mother's womb and be born again?" (vs. 4).

If we are to have the right understanding of what Jesus meant, we must hold in our minds the fact that the new birth is given to us as an analogy with physical birth. The new birth is indeed a new life, but it comes from the Word of God. "This Word goes into the womb of the heart where faith lays hold upon it. By this contact of faith and the Word there comes forth a new life. It is as real as physical life. It is entirely different from physical life. It is eternal life. It is spiritual life. It is abundant life. By this union of the Word and faith within our hearts we have become sons of God." [1]

THE ULTIMATE OPERATION

Jesus' reference to the wind (vss. 5–8) means the Holy Spirit, who effects the new birth in the deceitful and wicked heart of man. This has been likened to the surgery performed by Dr. Christiaan Barnard, who made amazing strides in the history of medical science with the first heart-transplant operation. *Time* Magazine called that "The Ultimate Operation." When the Holy Spirit gives new life from heaven, it is a work of God, the Great Physician—*the* ultimate operation to give us who are dying of "progressive heart failure" a *new* heart pulsing with divine life.

THE BEWILDERED PROFESSIONAL TEACHER

Poor Nicodemus! We see him groping for words as he blurts out, "How can this be? What do you mean?" (vs. 9). The great "teacher of Israel" stands before the despised

[1] Donald Grey Barnhouse, *The Love Life* (Glendale, Calif.: Regal Books Division, G/L Publications, 1973) p. 35.

Prophet from Galilee, seeking for light, and receives teaching that sends his mind reeling in blind incredulity and astonishment.

Patiently, Jesus outlines to Nicodemus the offer that God makes to all men; nothing less, indeed, than membership in the family of God. Nicodemus remembers all the things Jesus says and is later guided by those words ringing in his ears.

Jesus takes a story from Old Testament history—which story Nicodemus recognizes—and uses it to portray his death upon the cross:

> "For only I, the Messiah, have come to earth and will return to heaven again. And as Moses in the wilderness lifted up the bronze image of a serpent on a pole, even so I must be lifted up upon a pole, so that anyone who believes in me will have eternal life" (vss. 13–15).

Nicodemus, like all other devout Jews, was looking for the coming of the Messiah; and now, here is Jesus telling Nicodemus that he is that One, and that his death would mean Nicodemus' life. He explains this peculiar plan of salvation in what has often been called the "Miniature Gospel," because there is a sense in which the whole story of the Bible is spelled out in it.

> "For God so loved the world, that he gave his only begotten Son, that whosoever believeth in him should not perish, but have everlasting life" (vs. 16 AV).

There is no other more all-embracing word than "whosoever." It includes us. It included Nicodemus that day, and we know that he did become a follower of Jesus, for we see him later openly assisting in Jesus' burial.

How important it is to read that verse and realize what it is saying. It says, "that whosoever believeth in him should not perish, but have everlasting life." That is present possession. It does not say, *"hope* to have everlasting life."

A little boy said one day, "Faith is believing God and asking no questions." We don't read of Nicodemus asking Jesus any more questions nor of his raising any more doubts. This very religious man, this leader in both the political and religious life of his nation, had to come to the point where he evidenced childlike faith. Ask no more questions, my friend reading this, but demonstrate that kind of faith yourself. You, too, can be born again.

7

Restoration of a Woman:
Jesus as the True Emancipator

The Text: John 4:1–42
The Place: Jacob's Well, near the City of Sychar in Samaria
The Event: Jesus' Conversation with the Woman at the Well

One of the old rabbinical rules stated: "Let no one talk with a woman in the street, no not with his own wife." This was one of hundreds of such ordinances designed to keep women under subjugation. The entrenched view of Jesus' day was that women were secondary creatures. Jesus lived in what has rightly been called a totally patriarchal society. A woman was regarded mainly as a breeder and chattel, to be subject to her male master. A maxim of the times reads: "Blessed is he whose children are males, and woe to him whose children are females." (Where did these pious, "superior" men think males would come from if women suddenly stopped giving birth to females!) If ever sexist prejudice existed, it did so at the time Jesus came upon the scene. If ever women had a right to rise up in protest, it was then.

Jesus always showed special concern for the downtrodden, and in John 4 we see him doing a most astonishing thing—astonishing, that is, considering the status of that most disparaged of all classes, women.

> Jesus left Judea and returned to the province of Galilee.
> He had to go through Samaria on the way, and around

noon as he approached the village of Sychar, he came to Jacob's Well, located on the parcel of ground Jacob gave to his son Joseph. Jesus was tired from the long walk in the hot sun and sat wearily beside the well. Soon a Samaritan woman came to draw water, and Jesus asked her for a drink. He was alone at the time as his disciples had gone into the village to buy some food. The woman was surprised that a Jew would ask a "despised Samaritan" for anything —usually they wouldn't even speak to them!—and she remarked about this to Jesus (John 4:3–9).

CAN YOU IMAGINE A TIRED, DUSTY, AND THIRSTY JESUS?

Not only was Jesus divine, he was human. As such, he was subject to the same reaction to long travel (walking) as you or I would be. But what wondrous grace that he, the eternal God, so linked himself with our humanity that he should know what weariness meant. When you are tired, you can tell Jesus about it, and ask him for renewed strength and help. Jesus knows the heart of a weary man or woman.

John tells us that Jesus *had to go* through Samaria. Geographically speaking, he really didn't have to do anything of the kind, because there were two alternate routes. An orthodox Jew would take a circuitous route to avoid a confrontation with the "despised Samaritans." But Jesus was not a stern legalist. Jesus' action in traveling through Samaria was a "must" that had been decreed in heaven, settled in the counsels of eternity, long before the creation of the world.

Hostility was rising up against him in Judea; the religious leaders in Jerusalem, blinded by prejudice, pride, and willful sinfulness stubbornly refused to recognize who he was. He chose the road they would never take as a protest against their reason for not taking it. It would prove to be an indication of the inclusiveness of his Messiahship. Jesus was forever overstepping the narrow boundaries of Hebrew prejudice. Repeatedly, we see him acting to challenge it.

The disciples went on into the village for food, but Jesus

stayed behind, sitting by Jacob's well. As he sat there, looking across the beautiful countryside and the olive green valley, his meditation was broken by the appearance of a Samaritan woman.

JESUS AND THE WOMAN OF ILL REPUTE

Jesus was every bit as much at ease with women as he was with men. It is most generally agreed that the fact that this woman came to the well alone, at the sixth hour (probably high noon and the hottest part of the day, the most unlikely time to be drawing water), is an indication that she was a woman with a bad reputation, a scarlet woman. She would seek to avoid the contempt and scorn of the townspeople and so she would venture out then. But Jesus treated this one, considered to be at the bottom of the scrap heap of humanity, with as much consideration as he had shown to the respected Nicodemus.

Dr. Paul Tournier refers to what he calls the *personalism* of the Bible in many of his writings. God said to Moses, for instance, "I know you by name" (Ex. 33:17); and in this encounter with the Samaritan woman, knowing all about her and her past history and present sinful life, Jesus throws a bridge across the gulf that lay between her and him by asking her for a drink of water. We see mingled tact and condescension. The love of God is so completely universal, yet so beautifully and completely individual. Augustine expressed it well: "God loves each one of us as if there was only one of us to love." Truly, with God there is no one who is lost in the crowd.

In spite of this woman's bad record and low reputation, Jesus chose her as the recipient of his second great lesson. Here we see the pure grace of God, the God who gives. It is a dramatic scene.

There is something far worse than a thirsty throat: it is a thirsty heart. Jesus felt the dryness of the woman's parched soul more than his own parched mouth. He forgot his weariness and thirst in his joy at the thought of this shriveled-up soul becoming fresh with the wonderful water he alone could supply.

MOTIVATED BY LOVE

The woman at the well has been described as a seeking, seductive, lonesome, passionate woman of dalliance, a cast-off of five men and living unmarried with a sixth; nevertheless, Jesus asks a favor of her. She is accustomed to having men request favors—but what they seek is far different, and the manner of Jesus' approach, the tone of his voice, everything about him reveals this difference to her. How courteous he is, his smile so kind. Jesus' request is a manifestation of divine strategy and of psychological insight.

The woman is in for some surprises. Jesus is going to give a glorious *mashal* (or riddlelike saying). It will cause reflection, wonderment—exactly what Jesus wants.

> "If you only knew what a wonderful gift God has for you, and who I am, you would ask me for some *living* water!"
>
> "But you don't have a rope or a bucket," she said, "and this is a very deep well! Where would you get this living water? And besides, are you greater than our ancestor Jacob? How can you offer better water than this which he and his sons and cattle enjoyed?"
>
> Jesus replied that people soon became thirsty again after drinking this water. "But the water I give them," he said, "becomes a perpetual spring within them, watering them forever with eternal life" (vss. 10–14).

Jesus appeals to the inner craving everyone has for ultimate rest and satisfaction. Jesus does not demean her, he does not frighten her off, and now it is she who is asking a favor of him. She blurts out, "Please, sir, give me some of that water! Then I'll never have to make this long trip out here every day" (vs. 15).

Jesus addresses himself to her conscience: "Go and get your husband" (vs. 16).

REACTION OF THE SO-CALLED "EMANCIPATED WOMAN"

What? Had she heard him correctly? Get her husband? Why that of all things? Immediately she is evasive; she wants no interference from him along those lines. She is an emancipated woman. So she thought. How many there are like her today—fearful of being discovered for what they really are, wearing masks, defenses always up, but bleeding inside, so wounded, hurt and lonely. Her reply? "But I'm not married." She has thrown up her guard, but Jesus will not leave her alone. He will finish what he has begun.

> "All too true!" Jesus said. "For you have had five husbands, and you aren't even married to the man you're living with now" (vs. 18).

The stranger's résumé of her evil life shocks her beyond telling. It is not at all unusual for someone to try and change the subject in the course of a conversation if they wish to divert the channel of talk. The Samaritan woman makes this attempt; she is anxious for him to drop this painful subject:

> "Sir," the woman said, "you must be a prophet. But say, tell me, why is it that you Jews insist that Jerusalem is the only place of worship, while we Samaritans claim it is here (at Mount Gerazim) where our ancestors worshipped?" (vss. 19, 20).

The woman's mistake is a common one. Religion is more than form and ceremony; more than a place, it is a Person. It is not the *where* but the *how* and the *what* that is all-important.

> Jesus saith unto her, "Woman, *believe me* [italics author's], the hour cometh, when ye shall neither in this mountain, nor yet at Jerusalem, worship the Father. Ye worship ye know not what: we know what we worship: for salvation is of

the Jews. But the hour cometh, and now is when the true worshippers shall worship the Father in spirit and in truth: for the Father seeketh such to worship him. God is a Spirit: and they that worship him must worship *him* in spirit and in truth" (vss. 21–24 AV).

Jesus directs her thoughts toward the expected Messiah. It is deliberate.

MESSIANIC SELF-DISCLOSURE

"Well, at least I know that the Messiah will come—the one they call Christ—and when he does, he will explain every-think to us." Then Jesus told her, "I am the Messiah!" (vss. 25, 26).

The supreme moment of Messianic self-disclosure had arrived. The startling declaration from the lips of Jesus leaves her speechless! The woman at the well looks into those wonderful eyes of Jesus, still wordless, and, leaving behind her waterpot, rushes back to the village. She came thirsty, but, I believe, she left satisfied.

God's timing is *so* right. Just then his disciples arrive. They are surprised to find him talking to a woman and they receive a lesson in the true emancipation of womanhood at that moment.

MESSIAH!

I am sure this woman ran all the way back to the village, her legs couldn't carry her fast enough. If I had been she, I'd have repeated the word Messiah over and over. Always before, she had gone to any means to avoid a confrontation with the townspeople; but not now. We are told that she tells every-one, "Come and meet a man who told me everything I ever did! Can this be the Messiah?" (vs. 29).

Here is this woman of ill repute making this statement, actually admitting to her bad past, and the people drop everything and listen. It must have had something to do with the transformation of her very countenance that the meeting with Christ did to her. She is a changed woman. There will always be a change when Christ enters the heart of a sinner. The people see it. Not only do they listen, but, the Bible says, "So the people came streaming from the village to see him" (vs. 30).

It is incredible! Yet it happened! Can Jesus use those who have failed so miserably in the past? Does past failure disqualify one for future usefulness? *Jesus had a new disciple, a new follower, and a woman at that!* Notice the woman of Samaria at work for Jesus. The testimony of the many-times married and divorced woman resulted, the Bible says, in many believing he was the Messiah "because of the woman's report" (vs. 39).

The Samaritan woman was saved. And there was a wonderful awakening in the village because of her testimony. Whenever God saves a soul, it is in order that the saved one may share God's great love and mercy with somebody else. If we have had our thirst satisfied by this Living Water, then Jesus would have us tell others.

HARVESTTIME

The disciples gather with Jesus at the well and prepare to share the food with him only to hear him say, "My nourishment comes from doing the will of God who sent me, and from finishing his work" (vs. 34). As the Samaritans approach Jesus directs the disciples' attention to the arriving procession: "Look around you! Vast fields of human souls are ripening all around us, and are ready now for reaping" (vs. 35b).

Just a few moments before, the seed had been sown by Jesus in the heart of the woman, then by her in the hearts of the people. How quickly harvesttime can arrive! When Jesus sent the disciples to the village, all they did was buy some food; but Jesus saved a harlot, and she brought back the whole town!

8

The Second Sign:
Distance Is No Barrier to the Power of Christ

The Text: John 4:43–54
The Place: Cana in Galilee
The Event: Encounter with the Nobleman and Healing of
his Son

Distance is no barrier to the power of Christ. If ever there
was an appeal of agony from the lips of a parent, this was it.
If you heard of a physician who specialized in miracles and
you had a little one at the point of death, what would you do?
You'd probably do what the nobleman did. If you couldn't
move the child, you'd go to the miracle worker and try to
get him to come and heal your loved one.

> In the course of his journey through Galilee Jesus arrived
> at the town of Cana, where he had turned the water into
> wine. While he was there, a man in the city of Capernaum,
> a government official, whose son was very sick, heard that
> Jesus had come from Judea and was traveling in Galilee.
> This man went over to Cana, found Jesus, and begged him
> to come to Capernaum with him and heal his son, who was
> now at death's door (John 4:46, 47).

The fame of Jesus had spread far and wide. When word
reached this royal officer, he quickly came to Jesus, pleading
for him to return to Capernaum. This man could have sent a

servant, but he came himself, so great was his desire to get Jesus to come and perform a miracle upon his son.

THE RICH HAVE PROBLEMS AS WELL AS THE POOR

Money is not almighty. It cannot buy back lost health. The nobleman knew this. You can be sure he had not spared any expense in trying to procure restoration of health for this precious son. The rich have problems as well as the poor. Rich or poor, we can bring our problems to Jesus.

Sadness, anxiety, and sickness can bring us to Christ; and even though we have turned our backs, and ignored him, he will not turn his back on us when we do come to him, driven there in the hour of our extremity.

Sickness and sorrow, anxiety and trouble, can be blessings in disguise. If the nobleman's son had never been ill, his father and his whole house might have lived and died in their sins.

JESUS WILL NOT BE HURRIED

The nobleman was concerned that Jesus might not get to his son in time. But Jesus will not be hurried. We cannot bribe, force, or coerce him in any way.

Vast numbers of people think of God as though his great business is only to help us—whether we are sick, in a financial mess, or need some temporal benefit. But there is something higher than that in this matter of believing faith. God has purposes deeper than the comfort of sorrow or the healing of the sick. He would have us to know that he who is God became Man; and in getting to know him, the Son, we know the Father. "This is life eternal, that they might know Thee, the only true God, and Jesus Christ, whom thou hast sent."

Jesus had to show this to the nobleman. At first reading, Jesus' answer to the man's anguished plea seems harsh: "Won't any of you believe in me unless I do more and more miracles?" (vs. 48). But those were Jesus' words.

Jesus wasn't going to refuse to answer the father's anguished plea, but the man had to believe *in* Jesus, not just in miracles.

LIFE ACTS IN RESPONSE TO FAITH

The nobleman took the reproof of Jesus very graciously. He spoke to Christ respectfully, even though he was burdened with grief while his son hovered between life and death. He was soon to learn that distance of time and place are no obstructions to the power of Jesus. Jesus didn't need to go to Capernaum to heal the son.

> Then Jesus told him, "Go back home. Your son is healed!" And the man believed the word that Jesus had spoken unto him, and he went his way (vs. 50).

The nobleman didn't press Christ any further. We have here a beautiful portrait of the importance of taking Christ at his word.

BELIEVING IS AS GOOD AS SEEING

Jesus created an opportunity for the exercise of faith, although there was no outward visible sign. Let us know for a certainty that in the things of God, believing is as good as seeing.

> When he was on his way, some of his servants met him with the news that all was well—his son had recovered. He asked them when the lad had begun to feel better, and they replied, "Yesterday afternoon at about one o'clock his fever suddenly disappeared!" Then the father realized it was the same moment that Jesus had told him, "Your son is healed." And the officer and his entire household believed that Jesus was the Messiah" (vss. 51–53).

Though Jesus is in heaven, *we* are not separated by distance or time from him. He hears our cries. He meets our needs. The Son of God can assert his will on your behalf. Do you have the faith to believe *in* him?

PART II

Public Ministry

9

The Third Sign:
Jesus Equal with God?

The Text: John 5
The Place: Jerusalem
The Event: Healing of the Man at the Bethesda Pool

Christ is always tenderly inquisitive concerning the sick and suffering. This is nowhere more evident than at the place called the Bethesda Pool. It had five covered porches where great numbers of sick folk lay, waiting for the movement of the water. It was the ancient belief that supernatural virtue emanated from the water when, from time to time, an angel would come down and move the water. The first person who was quick enough to touch the moving surface after these angelic visitations was supposed to receive healing.

JESUS THE GREAT PHYSICIAN IN ACTION

One of the men lying there had been sick for thirty-eight years. When Jesus saw him and knew how long he had been ill, he asked him, "Would you like to get well?" (John 5:5, 6).

Jesus saw, knew, and acted. It was a singularly beautiful, unforced bit of kindness. The man hadn't cried out for help. But Christ was very much aware of this man's condition; just as he is of any of his children today. There came from the

49

lips of Jesus a quick, sharp, threefold command: "Rise, take up thy bed, and walk" (vs. 8 AV).

> Instantly the man was healed! He rolled up the mat and began walking! (vs. 9).

But one thing stands out glaringly! It was on the Sabbath that this miracle was done. So the Jewish leaders objected (vs. 9b). Of course, what did you expect? Surely not approval; surely not from these legalists gladness and great joy that this poor wretched creature was now freed from his misery!

LEGALISM CAN VOICE RESISTANCE, BUT IT CANNOT STOP THE FLOW OF GOD'S MERCY

Notice these "righteous" Pharisees in action (as contrasted with Jesus' action):

> They said to the man who was cured, "You can't work on Sabbath! It's illegal to carry that sleeping mat!"
> "The man who healed me told me to," was his reply. "Who said such a thing as that?" they demanded. The man didn't know, and Jesus had disappeared into the crowd (vss. 10–13).

What a sinister thing it is to be so bound by law that a person cannot reach out with human love and kindness. Friendless, helpless, and hopeless, the man had laid near the wonder-working waters year after year, but derived no benefit from them. Neglected, overlooked, and forgotten, he was still observed by the all-seeing eye of Christ. A more public demonstration of Sabbath-breaking could hardly be imagined.

The Bible says that the Sabbath was made for man and that "the Son of man is Lord also of the sabbath" (Mark 2:27, 28). Works of mercy and of real necessity to man's life and animal existence were never intended to be forbidden.

Legalists have their successors in every age and place. But what a warning is contained in this chapter to faultfinders and those who set themselves up as judges always looking for grounds for accusation. Elsewhere, with stinging rhetoric, Jesus lashes out at the outward righteousness and inward corruption of these same men: "Woe to you, Pharisees, and you religious leaders—hypocrites!"

Woe! Woe to *all* religious pretenders. What Jesus said needs no additional commentary!

JESUS ON A COLLISION COURSE!

Understandably, Jesus' popularity took a decided downward course. This act of healing precipitated a conflict with the Pharisees that soon became a roaring conflagration. From that point on, the leaders were anxious to do away with him. It was to be over a year before they succeeded, but their hearts were full of hatred and murderous thoughts now. This was cold, deliberate hatred, legalism at its very worst—sinful men, self-satisfied, full of pride, callous and cruel. Let it be clearly understood that these Pharisees were characterized by a dreadful devotion to the Sabbath and to all their laws, ready even to murder to defend their Sabbath restrictions.

But what happened to the man who was healed? He hadn't been inside the Temple for thirty-eight years, and that's where he headed and where Jesus found him. Jesus said to him, "Now you are well; don't sin as you did before, or something even worse may happen to you" (vs. 14). Jesus was saying that the misery from which he was made whole should serve as a warning. A sick bed is a sorrowful place, but hell is much worse! It was a "Go and sin no more" admonition.

The harassment of Jesus by the Jewish leaders now begins in earnest. From verse nineteen to the end of chapter five we hear Jesus speaking some of the most profound words he ever uttered. He asserts his Divine nature, his unity with God the Father, and the high dignity of his office. Of all the teachings that Jesus had to give, this was the farthest beyond human comprehension. Feeble men still have difficulty accepting the fact that the omnipotent Creator is our heavenly Father and that Jesus is his human Son, his equal. Even Jesus' disciples had difficulty reaching the first rung in this mental ladder.

A Jesus-like God

We have a Jesus-like God, a God who cares. In Jesus, God was providing the way for men to obtain salvation and eternal life. Jesus was the embodiment of the purposes of God. He was the Light of God, drawing men to the truth and to a better life in the here and now. In Jesus, a new dimension of love and mercy was given; but the legalists preferred to believe that the road to salvation was in keeping the law.

Over and over again we see Jesus using the words *verily, verily*. The meaning is "I say emphatically." He repeats his cooperation with God, and God's cooperation with him. His claims are stupendous.

> "Verily, verily, I say unto you, He that heareth my word, and believeth on him that sent me, hath everlasting life, and shall not come into condemnation; but is passed from death unto life" (vs. 24 AV).

Christ Knows Us Better Than We Know Ourselves

Jesus then moves on into another very touchy aspect of the problem as he makes reference to the Scriptures. Remember, he was speaking to men who had devoted their lives to the study of the Old Testament.

> "Ye search the Scriptures, for you believe they give you eternal life. And the Scriptures point to me! Yet you won't come to me so that I can give you this life eternal!" (vss. 39–40 AV).

He dares to tell them they will stand in judgment for their failure to accept him (vss. 40–47). There is satire in what he is saying. To search the Scriptures is needful, but not with a closed mind.

The folly of these men's position is shown, as is their ignorance of God. They miss what they seek because of their obstinacy and failure to follow the pathway through the Scriptures to the Source of Life—Jesus himself. Christ knows us better than we know ourselves. That is a sobering thought.

Jesus equal with God? Believe it and receive life eternal. It is *the* Word of a Man of his Word.

10

The Fourth and Fifth Signs and the First "I Am": The Adequacy of Christ's Provision

> The Place: John 6
> The Place: The Sea of Galilee
> The Event: Feeding of the Multitude; Stilling of the Storm and Jesus Walking on the Water; Jesus Teaching About the True Bread

Preoccupation with one's stomach (earthly-mindedness) at the expense of one's soul is risky business. This is not to say that problems and adverse circumstances (hunger and present-day needs) are not real and to be reckoned with (for indeed such situational difficulties cannot be glossed over as if they didn't exist), but it is to recognize that we don't come to Jesus only for mere handouts as if this was our just due.

> When Jesus went up into the hills and sat down with his disciples around him, he soon saw a great multitude of people climbing the hill, looking for him.
> Turning to Philip he asked, "Philip, where can we buy bread to feed all these people?" (He was testing Philip, for he already knew what he was going to do.)
> Philip replied, "It would take a fortune to begin to do it!" (John 6:3–7).

Jesus looks upon this vast sea of humanity and is concerned about their welfare. It is late in the day, time to eat, and everyone is tired and hungry.

THE PHILIP-LIKE SPIRIT

Philip estimated that it would take a day's pay of two hundred men to buy sufficient bread for the crowd. Weak faith, eyes closed to God's great miracle-working power, we too, look at the things we can see; like Philip, we calculate, but fail to take into account that we have a miracle-working Christ who cares about the things that concern us. Let us look at the lad and the Lord. Little is much when God is in it.

THERE ARE NO INSUPERABLE DIFFICULTIES WITH CHRIST

Often we distrust God's power when visible and ordinary means fail in our particular distressing circumstances; we fail to trust farther than what we can see.

Andrew had been scurrying around to see what he could find among the people in the way of food. Now he says, "There's a youngster here with five barley loaves and a couple of fish! But what good is that with all this mob?" (vs. 9). The Bible tells us that the approximate count of the men only was five thousand, not counting women and children.

Not only can Jesus heal, but he can do even greater than this: he can call into being that which was not before, and call it out of nothing.

I can't help but wonder how that little lad felt when Jesus took his five loaves and two fish. I can picture Jesus putting his arms around the little fellow, drawing him close, and saying, "Thank you for being willing to share; now don't you worry, there will be enough for you and everyone else. Just watch, we're going to have a big picnic out here, and no one is going to be hungry."

Then Jesus took the loaves and gave thanks to God and passed them out to the people. Afterwards he did the same with the fish. And everyone ate until full! "Now gather the scraps," Jesus told his disciples, "so that nothing is wasted." And twelve baskets were filled with leftovers! When the people realized what a great miracle had happened, they exclaimed, "Surely, he is the Prophet we have been expecting!" (vss. 11–14).

As fast as Jesus broke the loaves, so fast did the loaves multiply in his hands. There was a continual act of creation going on in the breaking of the loaves and the fish. The supply seemed inexhaustible, there was not just a morsel, a tempting taste for every person, but an abundant supply, enough and to spare.

The disciples went about afterwards gathering up twelve basketsful of leftovers.

After Jesus performed this miracle, the people were understandably tremendously impressed. Their reaction was a natural one; they wanted to make Jesus their king, and by force, if necessary. The situation came close to getting out of hand, an unusual thing in Jesus' life. It was a spontaneous movement on the part of the people. Jesus wanted no such honor; he sought no greatness for himself. He turned from this to the solitude of the mountains to pray. Evening was coming on, and Jesus sent his disciples to the water's edge.

MASTER OF EVERY STORM AND TEMPEST

One of the most famous squalls in history took place on the Sea of Galilee that night.

That evening his disciples went down to the shore to wait for him. But as darkness fell and Jesus hadn't come back, they got into the boat and headed out across the lake toward Capernaum. But soon a gale swept down upon them as they rowed, and the sea grew very rough (vss. 16–18).

Sudden and severe storms characterize the Sea of Galilee. Even though these men were fishermen and accustomed to the angry moods of the sea, the Bible tells us, "They were terrified."

Life is like that. Unpredicted storms come. Questions follow. Terror grips our heart. More questions. Has Jesus forgotten us? (Had he forgotten the disciples?) We are distressed. (They were distressed.) But Jesus had not deserted them, any more than he would desert you in your times of distress. In the tempest and darkness of life, Jesus is Light and hope and deliverance.

Added to their perplexity and disappointment over his refusal to be made king, was this new threat to their lives as they struggled in the face of the fierce wind. And then, out of the gloom of darkness and the wild storm they saw a figure approaching, walking, head against the contrary wind. The sea was raging, the wind violent. The disciples were afraid. The waves that threatened to engulf them were as pavement to his feet. He who created the world, and who controls the world, walked upon the water as though it were dry land. He would not leave his disciples comfortless; he will not leave you comfortless. He is the Master of every storm and tempest. Though you panic and are fearful, he calls out: "It is I; be not afraid" (vs. 20). When trouble is near, Jesus is nearer.

And so Jesus speaks to every anxious heart crying for help. There is no need to fall under the oppression of your difficulties. Just as Jesus saw the keenness of disappointment and the perplexity of the disciples as they crossed that sea in the darkness of the night, and he came to them, so he will come to you.

It was just as easy for Jesus to walk on the sea as it was to form the sea at the beginning. Our God is Lord of waves and winds, of storms and tempests, and he will come to his own in their darkest hour when faith is sorely tried. And when Jesus comes, there is calm.

When Jesus entered the ship, the Bible says, the boat reached the shore immediately. There is comfort and hope in that for us. With Christ in the vessel, we will reach port.

FROM TEMPORAL TO ETERNAL REALITIES

A man who could fill empty stomachs was a great attraction. The materialistic crowd was still anxious to find this wholesale-food provider (vss. 22–27), and they came across the lake the next morning. Preoccupation with their stomachs didn't deflect Jesus from speaking words of eternal truth. He was not going to bring in a new social order on a bread basis. Their priorities were wrong; their interest in him only superficial. Jesus, who can see the intents of a man's heart, knew that their interest in him was primarily temporal.

Jesus always fitted his teachings to the minds and hearts of his hearers. To these hard-working ordinary people he gave teaching that corresponded with their concern for the basic necessities of life. They were earthly-minded. Theirs was more the sin of indifference than anything else. Hungry people think about where their next meal is coming from.

Jesus went straight to the business on his heart. He rebuked their false interest; he wants no man's loyalty unless that man sees the love and truth of the Father in him. The tender love of Jesus stands out sharply against this background of human ingratitude.

Jesus told them, "This is the will of God, that you believe in the one he has sent." They replied, "You must show us more miracles if you want us to believe you are the Messiah. Give us free bread every day, like our fathers had while they journeyed through the wilderness! As the Scriptures say, 'Moses gave them bread from heaven.'" Jesus said, "Moses didn't give it to them. My Father did. And now he offers you true Bread from heaven. The true Bread is a Person—the one sent by God from heaven, and he gives life to the world."

"Sir," they said, "give us that bread every day of our lives!"

Jesus replied, "I am the Bread of Life. No one coming to me will ever be hungry again" (vss. 28–35).

What a tremendous proclamation! He has been fulfilling that promise for over nineteen hundred years.

What did he mean? To eat of the Bread of life is to receive him in faith, and then day by day to enjoy sweet communion with him through reading the Bible and meditating upon it as it reveals one marvelous truth after another. When one does this, he discovers that he loses his appetite for that which is unholy and sensuously wrong.

But how sense-bound were these people! They implied a disparaging comparison between Jesus and Moses. (Dead teachers have always more authority than living ones!) It is not want of evidence that keeps a man away from belief in Christ, it is want of heart. Plainly these people had not lacked for signs and proofs of Christ's Messiahship. How true it is that "none are so blind as those that will not see."

> Then the Jews began to murmur against him because he claimed to be the Bread from heaven.
>
> "What?" they exclaimed. "Why, he is merely Jesus the son of Joseph, whose father and mother we know. What is this he is saying, that he came down from heaven?" (vss. 41, 42).

How could one whose parents were known to these Galileans be from Heaven? Jesus' humanity posed a difficulty. Had he come as a conquering king, with wealth and honor, they would have willingly enough received him. But a poor, lowly, ordinary man? Reasoning has always been a great obstacle to belief in Christ. False conclusions about Christ, however, arise from imperfect knowledge about him and an unwillingness to open one's mind to receive the word of truth. Salvation does not come by comprehension of the mysteries of the Godhead; it is rather by simple faith in the Person of Christ.

Jesus continued to press his claims to be the Giver of eternal life (vss. 47–52).

> Then the Jews began arguing with each other about what he meant. "How can this man give us his flesh to eat?" they asked. (vs. 52).

Horrors! they were, in effect, saying. Why, this is cannibalism. To make matters worse, Jesus added the teaching about drinking his blood (vs. 53). The people were stunned. The final reaction of many in that audience that day was negative. "This is an hard saying, who can hear it?" (vs. 60b AV).

Jesus, of course, was speaking of an inward and spiritual act of the heart, and it had nothing to do with the body. It is laying hold on Christ, trusting in his atonement (death on the cross, resurrection, and ascension—we shall come to more of this in later chapters), and allowing one's soul to feed on Christ's sacrifice by faith. Acceptance of this lies at the root of Christianity. It is basic to salvation; it unites us to our Savior and entitles us to the privileges of being called a child of God, assuring us of access to the Father.

With the conclusion of this marvelous teaching, the Bible tells us that many of his disciples turned away and deserted him (vs. 66). They came to a parting of the ways. Evidently, it was quite a defection. Would the Twelve join the exodus? Then Jesus turned to the Twelve and asked, "Are you going too?" (vs. 67).

Jesus' question was intended as a further sifting of the ranks. With characteristic ardor, Peter answered: "Master, to whom shall we go? You alone have the words that give eternal life, and we believe them and know you are the holy Son of God" (vss. 68, 69).

11

Open Opposition and Attempted Arrest:
Jesus, the Grand Prescriber

The Text: John 7
The Place: Jerusalem
The Event: The Feast of Tabernacles

Jesus satisfies. Not only does he give and sustain, but he
satisfies. Jesus' prescriptions, taken as directed, can safely be
relied upon to lead a person from here to eternity.

The Jews' hostility toward Christ was becoming more intense. Controversy surged; there was much unrest. By now
Jesus had established a known pattern of faithful attendance
at the special Jewish feast days and celebrations. He had
stayed out of Judea because he knew the Jewish leaders were
plotting his death (John 7:1); he did not frustrate the
Father's plans by coming to Jerusalem prematurely. Thus,
though everyone around him was highly agitated, his friends
perplexed, his own brothers scoffing at him, he was calm,
poised, and in control.

The Jewish feast of Tabernacles was at hand. Jesus'
brethren urged him to go to Judea for this celebration:

> "Go where more people can see your miracles!" they
> scoffed. "You can't be famous when you hide like this! If
> you're so great, prove it to the world!" (vss. 3b, 4).

The revealing statement is made: For even his brothers
didn't believe in him (vs. 5).

This is the advice of worldly wisdom, of cynical unbelief, of human impatience. It shows the desperate hardness of man's heart, alienated from the Savior. It shows also that a man may be a Christian, and yet have family members who are not in sympathy and accord with his beliefs. Parental religious heritage is no substitute for a personal relationship with God through Christ. This cannot be acquired through some kind of spiritual osmosis, or something that rubs off from one member of the family to another. There was a latent sneer in the comment of Jesus' brothers. They were trying to push him into the limelight; but there was no yielding to temptation.

Jesus' unbelieving brothers must have been a cause for heartache. That speaks comfort. Perhaps someone reading this is suffering that peculiar kind of agony that comes to those whose loved ones despise their religious beliefs and their love for Christ. Take heart; pour out your heartache to Jesus. He understands and cares.

> Jesus answered first in words, but later in action: "It is not the right time for me to go now. But you can go anytime and it will make no difference, for the world can't hate you; but it does hate me, because I accuse it of sin and evil. You go on and I'll come later when it is the right time" (vss. 6–8).

Whenever reference is made like this to "time," it means the set season, the prearranged program of the Father. He didn't say he wasn't going, but what he did indicate was "not yet." Jesus' reference here to "the world" is revealing. He always regarded men from the viewpoint of their relation to God. For Jesus to link these men with "the world" is a terrible commentary. "The world" was hostile to Christ. The Bible tells us that "friendship of the world is enmity against God." Jesus came to transfer men from the ranks of his critics and enemies to the company of the committed, those who would be his friends and believers. He came to rescue them from the evil grip of the world.

In Jesus' statement to his brothers we have a revelation that explains the deadly enmity with which many regarded him and his message. The presence of Jesus then, and the work of the Holy Spirit in the lives of Christians today, makes the world feel uncomfortable. The Bible speaks of it as men preferring the darkness to the Light. They would have tolerated his opinions if he would have spared exposure of their sins.

GOD'S RESTRAINING POWER IS AVAILABLE

Midway through the festival, Jesus went up to the Temple and preached openly (vs. 14).

There followed much perplexity on the part of the people. The object of the rulers' bitter hostility was in their midst; yet the rulers did not lay hands on him. Jesus was in perfect safety in the midst of these his foes because God was caring for him.

Can you believe that God cares for you like that? Many are the testimonies of God's saints who have experienced this tender, watching care. I think of Corrie ten Boom, who was miraculously delivered from a German concentration camp and who, in her experiences as a "tramp for the Lord" (which she calls herself) has experienced God's intervention on her behalf time after time. God's restraining power is available today.

> Many among the crowds at the Temple believed on him. "After all," they said, "what miracles do you expect the Messiah to do that this man hasn't done?" (vs. 31).

Their reasoning was correct.

Once again, surrounded by the protecting power of God, though officers came to arrest him (vss. 32–34), these representatives of authority left empty-handed. Nothing happens in this world except by the eternal counsels of our Father, and according to his eternal plans. I like what Corrie ten

Boom says: "There are no problems in heaven, only plans."
And these plans include your life and mine.

Jesus was saying that day to those who sought to kill him
that hell itself is truth known too late. God is merciful, but
there is a limit even to God's mercy. It was as though he was
saying, Heaven is a place where the wicked cannot come.

One of the important rites that took place at the time of
this festival had to do with the Jewish custom of drawing
water from the pool of Siloam and carrying it in solemn
procession to the Temple. This symbolism was to remind the
people that God had supplied their need with water in the
wilderness, and that God had made promises through the
prophets that there would come the day when God would
pour out his blessing with rivers of water.

OVERAWED BY JESUS

It is believed that quite possibly as Jesus saw this ritual
being observed on the last day, the climax of the holidays,
he shouted to the crowds, "If anyone is thirsty, let him come
to me and drink." "This grand prescription of Christ, is the
secret of all saving Christianity." [1] "Jesus was claiming that
he was to be for all the weary, unsatisfied, thirsty world what
the riven rock had been for Israel of old. No greater claim
could be made, nor under more impressive circumstances.[2]

The crowd, and the officers sent to arrest Jesus, were
deeply moved by what he said. "He says such wonderful
things!" they mumbled. "We've never heard anything like
it" (vs. 46). If the combined evidence of Christians living
all over the world could be collected today, I am certain
they would say the same thing.

---

[1] J. C. Ryle, *Ryle's Expository Thoughts on the Gospels* (Grand Rapids,
Mich.: Zondervan Publishing House, Anniversary Edition), p. 471.
[2] Charles R. Erdman, *The Gospel of John* (Philadelphia: Westminster
Press, 1944), pp. 73, 74.

12

The Second "I Am" and Light Rejected:
Defender of the Weak

The Text: John 8
The Place: Jerusalem
The Event: Jesus' Encounter with the Woman Taken in
Adultery; Jesus' Controversy with the Pharisees

Jesus had the tenderest heart and gentlest lips in all the
world. He always moved at the impulse of the Father's Love.
Jesus, as Love in action, calls forth the same awe-inspiring
reaction today as he did the day he dealt with the woman
dragged before him who had been taken in the act of
adultery. Christ is Christianity's greatest credential. There
are three instances recorded in the Gospels of Jesus' dealings
with women who had made a misstep like this, and in each
case Jesus was exceedingly considerate. Jesus' heart always
ached in sympathy for those who were having a hard time
with their weak natures. God was merciful to this woman in
the thing in which she needed his mercy so that she could
rise to a newness of life. Only forgiveness—complete forgiveness as demonstrated by Christ—can liberate a person from
enslaving passion and sinful tendencies; and we must do
nothing less than what Jesus did if we are to help others
along the way. Jesus' actions and words in this encounter are
a rebuke to those today who have a standoffish attitude toward the weak and wayward, as if by being kind to them

and showing acceptance we somehow become tainted. It is a dangerous thing to pick up the sword of judgment.

JESUS DEFLATES THE RIGORISTS

Jesus returned to the Mount of Olives (John 8:1), following the events in the preceding chapter, to spend the night alone with God under the canopy of the heavens. The religious leaders held a council against him, how they might destroy him. That "Get Jesus Committee," as Barnhouse called them, had but one aim—they were determined to trip Jesus up somehow, and they didn't care what it might take to do it. They would impale him on the horns of a dilemma. The brutal indelicacy of their action exposes the meanness and cowardice of their own souls.

> Early the next morning Jesus was back again at the Temple. A crowd soon gathered, and he sat down and talked to them. As he was speaking, the Jewish leaders and Pharisees brought a woman caught in adultery and placed her out in front of the staring crowd (vss. 2, 3).

Charles L. Allen says that possibly she was standing there unclothed, since women are stoned while naked, and more than likely her garments had already been ripped off. The humiliation must have been very great.[1]

> "Teacher," they said to Jesus, "this woman was caught in the very act of adultery. Moses' law says to kill her. What about it?" (vss. 4, 5).

These self-righteous custodians of morality with smug insolence fling this woman in front of him, and not in front of him only, but also the vast, gaping crowd who had gathered early to absorb more of Jesus' teachings. What a spectacle!

[1] See the author's book *Forgiveness in Action* (Hawthorn) for additional commentary on this episode in the life of Christ.

They had failed the day before in snaring Jesus, but now they used a more subtle approach. These "lovers" of the law determined to try to trap Jesus into saying something they could use against him (vs. 6). If he said she was to go free, he would be contradicting the Mosaic Law. If he said she was to be stoned, he would be involving himself with the Roman authorities. The attempt was shrewdly calculated to make Christ act contrary to either the ecclesiastical or civil law. They thought they could catch Jesus coming or going!

George W. Cornell, Associated Press religion writer, has recreated the scene that shows vividly the dramatic and deeply significant confrontation. "Jesus eyed the waiting circle of hard, disdainful male faces, thirsting for violence against this errant, disheveled woman at their feet. He knew their objective. . . . However, only a man's word counted legally and so women generally became the sole culprits.

"The world then, akin to the present, tolerated a dual morality, a double stardard, in which men's philandering was unlawful but disregarded, while the straying woman was irredeemably condemned." [2]

(One is tempted to ask the question as to how these "respectable" men knew where to find this "sinful" woman. Did Jerusalem have a red-light district, or did one or more of the men have her "number" up their sleeve?)

EXIT THE EXECUTIONERS

The woman's accusers stooped so low as to take a woman (why didn't they grab the man? If she was "caught in the act," as they claimed, then the man had to be there) and use her as a club to strike at Christ. But Jesus "stooped down and wrote in the dust with his finger" (vs. 6b). Jesus will always stoop low to help the fallen sinner.

The act and reply of Jesus is unmatched in beauty and wisdom. There are those even today who seem to take a special sort of sadistic delight in another's shame. Charles R.

[2] *Philadelphia Inquirer,* April 10, 1974.

Erdman says: "That they (the Jewish leaders and Pharisees) should be willing to form a plot so distressing and repulsive shows that they were ready to stoop to any measure in order to accomplish their desired end. We find that the character of men is often revealed by the instruments which they employ to secure their purposes. . . . They may not have been guilty of the particular sin in question, although possibly our Lord referred to the fact that impure thoughts are sinful as well as impure deeds; but they were guilty of sin. . . . Jesus teaches that men who wish to assume for themselves the function of official judges must themselves be pure." [3]

If the woman was standing there trembling and naked, I would imagine Jesus' first act was to cover her nakedness. He would, no doubt, have turned to the crowd and asked someone to drape something around her. The writer of Psalms expresses it so well when he says, "Blessed is he whose transgression is forgiven, whose sin is covered" (Ps. 32:1). "Forgiveness is the cloak for our naked, sinful souls." [4]

Jesus covers us with his love. He covered the woman taken in adultery with that love.

Many legends have been handed down as to what Jesus wrote when he traced his finger in the dust. But they are all speculative. The fact is we simply do not know. Whatever it was, the words Jesus uttered—"All right, hurl the stones at her until she dies. But only he who never sinned may throw the first!" (vs. 7b)—had the desired effect.

Jesus showed that he and he alone is qualified to rightfully judge all men; by this action and utterance he silenced, convicted, and condemned his enemies and the woman's. It was as if he said, "Look, you self-appointed executors of divine justice, if you want to take the place of God, then make certain your lives are just as pure." G. Campbell Morgan says that sentence put him out of the stone-throwing business for the rest of his life!

[3] *The Gospel of John,* pp. 76, 77.
[4] Charles L. Allen, *The Touch of the Master's Hand* (Old Tappan, N.J.: Fleming H. Revell Co., ₁₉66), p. 106.

Then Jesus stooped down again and wrote some more in the dust. And the Jewish leaders slipped away one by one, beginning with the eldest, until only Jesus was left in front of the crowd with the woman (vss. 8, 9).

Jesus' penetrating gaze went right through those men. There wasn't a one of them who was morally qualified to do what the group had set out to do. "They hesitated, pinioned within their own private delinquencies, glancing about at each other, waiting for someone else to hurl that lordly missile of self-acclaiming spotlessness. At length one of them, shaking his head, turned away, and the stone slid from his hand. Gradually the others, eyes cast down, silently did the same, the stones falling to the ground, a muffled, uneven clunking in the stillness." [5]

Exit the executioners. These men did not dare to take away a life with their hands that they had already tried to take away with their tongues. "Undetected crime has no authority to cast stones at crime detected." [6]

What a lesson! We who have such limited knowledge and understanding of the heart and life of another cannot claim the right to point even an accusing finger at someone else.

In the glaring light of the Light of the world, the woman's accusers retreated.

Eugenia Price believes the woman taken in adultery sinned because she was hungry for love. She believes the woman caught in this act did not run away (she could have after her accusers left) because she was seeking love, and in Jesus she recognized love personified. She waited because, standing before him, she saw not only the sin in her own life but the hope for her in his forgiveness. And this is what forgiveness does for an individual—it opens up doors of hope. "It has been said that the most redeemable person alive is the one who has sinned seeking love." [7]

[5] George W. Cornell, *Philadelphia Inquirer,* April 10, 1974.
[6] G. Campbell Morgan, *The Analysed Bible* (London: Hodder and Stoughton, 1909), p. 123.
[7] Eugenia Price, *The Unique World of Women* (Grand Rapids, Mich.: Zondervan Publishing House, 1969), p. 210.

ONLY JESUS

Then Jesus stood up again and said to her, "Where are your accusers? Didn't even one of them condemn you?"
"No, sir," she said.
And Jesus said, "Neither do I. Go and sin no more" (vss. 10, 11).

It was a case of Incarnate Purity standing confronting convicted impurity. The woman's name is not recorded; Jesus would afford her the mercy of anonymity. I am certain that she looked at Jesus through tear-dimmed eyes, with a quiver in her voice.

With one grand stroke of compassionate caring, God had erased from the Book of Life her sorry record of sin and sinning. This is God's prerogative. The Apostle Paul in his letter to the Romans amplifies on this idea by reminding us that the court of heaven is the only proper court for trial.

Psychologists tell us that the three basic needs of every human being are: first, the need to belong; second, the need for significance; third, the need for reasonable security. Jesus did not condone adultery, nor did he make a detour around the Law, but he gave his pardon and his love to this woman. He gave her back her self-respect and much more. He put within her heart the desire to live for him and to sin no more. What Malcom Muggeridge, the British journalist, said is so appropriate to describe this woman's liberation: "Christ is the only liberator whose liberation lasts forever." [8]

It should be noted that this passage is highly controversial. Many textual critics, including some evangelical scholars, question its right to existence because it does not appear in a number of the most significant early manuscripts of the Gospel of John. However, early biblical textual critics literally fought to retain it because it was their view that perhaps more than any other incident in the life of Christ, this en-

[8] *Jesus Rediscovered* (Wheaton, Ill.: Tyndale House Publishers, 1971), p. 6.

counter epitomized the all-embracing tender love of Jesus toward the sinner. (As late as 1611 scholars wrestled with the problem, calling upon the Holy Spirit for guidance, and therefore included it in their edition that became known as the Authorized King James Version. For that reason it is in our Bible as we know it today.) The critics feared that this would teach people to treat sin lightly; on the contrary, however, "We see it, not as a light treatment of sin, but as a tremendous illustration of salvation and righteousness, which is what the Lord intended it to be." [9]

THE LIGHT THAT LIGHTETH EVERY MAN

"I am the light of the world: he that followeth me shall not walk in darkness, but shall have the light of life" (vs. 12).

Jesus' statement implies that the world needs light; morally and spiritually it is in a dark condition. Jesus dares to declare himself to be the only remedy. There have always been false lights in the world leading men astray, but Jesus is the Light that lighteth every man. Jesus promised that to those who followed him, living light would flood their path. There would be no more stumbling through the darkness.

Once again the Pharisees rise up to accuse him of boasting and lying (vs. 13), but Jesus calmly asserts that his claims are true. The stormy debate continues—a discussion that included, among other things, parentage and pedigree. They demand that he tell them who his Father is as they, with a superior air, claim Abrahamic descent (vss. 14–47).

Jesus' analysis of their deteriorated character enrages these Pharisees. The fiery debate flames into an intensely heated verbal battle. Mark carefully what Jesus says: Love to Christ is the infallible mark of all true children of God, those who would claim God as their Father. There is a belief widely held that God is a universal Father. It is true that God

9 Donald Grey Barnhouse, p. 112.

the Father is full of love, mercy, and compassion, and that he is a seeking Savior; but he is not the spiritual Father of anyone who does not come to him through Christ. To say that God is your Father when you do not believe in and love Christ is to fall into the same error that these contending Jews did in this place.

I think it must have grieved Jesus' heart very much that day to see Abraham's descendants despising him. Jesus tells them that Abraham knew he was coming and was glad and rejoiced (vs. 56). He places Abraham and himself in proper perspective, but they only use it as fresh ground for scorn. "Before Abraham was, I am" (vs. 58). He claims eternity of existence, antedating even Abraham. It is too much. He is an impudent blasphemer as far as they are concerned. Snarling at him, they take up stones to kill him (vs. 59). "But Jesus was hidden from them, and walked past them and left the Temple" (vs. 59).

How does Jesus respond to their unbelief? He demonstrates his Deity by passing through their midst unseen. Can you picture their bewilderment? "Where is he?" "Where'd he go?" and they look about confused and dazed. We don't know if Jesus became invisible, or if God momentarily blinded the eyes of these enemies. What happened is not important; the important thing right now is, can you see? Do you understand? Listen to Jesus' words: "Unless you believe that I am the Messiah, the Son of God, you will die in your sins" (vs. 24).

13

The Sixth Sign and the Breach with Religious Leaders: Jesus and His Enemies

The Text: John 9
The Place: Jerusalem
The Event: Restoration of Sight to the Man Born Blind

It is possible to retrogress spiritually by holding blindly to tradition. There are worse things than physical blindness. How many there are pursuing their way blindly through life, obstinately determined to shut their eyes against light.

The theme of Jesus' life was to help those who needed help. Jesus explained his mission like this:

> "I must work the work of him that sent me, while it is day: the night cometh, when no man can work. As long as I am in the world, I am the light of the world" (John 9:4, 5 AV).

Jesus always did more than theorize about God. In the presence of pain, suffering, and need, his concern was to do something. A great part of Jesus' earthly ministry required his giving attention to congenital blindness. But the greater light that came in the incident in John 9 has to do with the illumination of the man's soul. One who once saw not, sees; but those who imagined themselves as being clear-sighted are found blind.

Jesus was not a divine health department, but

> As he was walking along, he saw a man blind from birth (vs. 1).

That stopped Jesus in his tracks.

Certainly it can be said that blindness is one of the saddest of all physical handicaps. To be deprived of one's sight would mean to be cut off from some of the greatest enjoyments of life. Try to imagine what it would be like never to see the face of loved ones, or a sunset, green grass, a harvest moon, fluffy white clouds in a deep blue sky, or any of the innumerable sights that you take for granted.

Others saw this man, but not as Jesus saw him. He was probably sitting near the Temple gateway to attract worshipers and receive alms.

THE GREAT X IN THE EQUATION OF LIFE

Jesus' eyes fell upon the blind man, and the disciples, noting his concerned look, asked him:

> "Master, why was this man born blind? Was it a result of his own sins or those of his parents?" (vs. 2).

There you have the great X in the equation of life. It is a question that has mystified millions and is repeatedly asked. But notice Jesus' answer to the disciples:

> "Neither hath this man sinned, nor his parents: but that the works of God should be made manifest in him" (vs. 3 AV).

It has been suggested by many wise ancient philosophers that the best way to answer the question of the origin of evil is to consider the end of it—"What good comes out of it?" This makes the subject plain and useful. When we philosophize in this way, then we can find light, certainty, and comfort. The mystery of evil is a problem I cannot solve, nor can you. As Christians, we know that many of life's most valuable lessons are spelled out with tears and suffering, and that triumph can issue forth from trouble. Barnhouse says, "God is not up in heaven trying to hit people. God is love."

Christ wasted no time in giving sight to the blind man. He said to the disciples, "While I am still here in the world, I give it my light" (vs. 5).

EFFORT DEMANDED

The lesson is obvious: in the presence of pain and suffering and worldwide need, it is our solemn responsibility as light-bearers to do something while there is time.

> Then he spat on the ground and made mud from the spittle and smoothed the mud over the blind man's eyes, and told him, "Go and wash in the Pool of Siloam" (the word "siloam" means "Sent"). So the man went where he was sent and washed and came back seeing! (vss. 6, 7).

There was no special virtue in the mud that could cure a man born blind. God is not bound in his methods of dealing with bodies or souls. You can expect him always to use a variety of means to make men whole. With or without means, the point to remember is that it is God who heals. I appreciate the comment of a doctor who said, "I only bandage men's wounds; God heals them."

Jesus' command to the man was a test of faith; in obedience the man received his sight. It is the same great principle that runs throughout the Bible: believe and obey. If we want to see the power of Christ operate in our lives, we must trust (have faith) and obey.

The blind man's family, friends, and others who knew him were so shocked they couldn't believe their eyes. But the once-blind man sets them straight: "I *am* the same man!" (vs. 9b), he joyfully declares, "And I *can* see!" ([italics author's] vs. 11b).

The domination of the Pharisees over the people was so strong that, rather than rejoicing with the man over this miraculous thing that had happened to him, the people take him to the religious leaders.

> Now as it happened, this all occurred on a Sabbath (vs. 14).

INTERROGATION

Then the Pharisees asked him all about it. So he told them how Jesus had smoothed the mud over his eyes, and when it was washed away, he could see! (vs. 15).

The blind-hearted enemies of Christ could see no beauty in the act; they failed "to see" the man, they were only concerned with the method (vs. 16). *Now* who was blind!

We have consistently seen what part the Sabbath observance played in the religion of the Pharisees; it had become an idol. We have also seen the authority and position these religious leaders took to themselves without regard to human dignity or showing of mercy. Jesus would break down such false idols.

> Then the Pharisees turned on the man who had been blind and demanded, "This man who opened your eyes—who do you say he is?"
> "I think he must be a prophet sent from God," the man replied (vs. 17).

At this stage in the man's interrogation the rulers called in his parents. Who could better identify the man? Can you imagine how the parents felt? Can you imagine how the man felt? Remember, he had never seen their faces until that day. Could he read the anxiety in their eyes? Did he see the fear in their hearts as it gave expression on their faces? Did he know that mothers always hurt for their children in a way that is peculiar to them alone? Did he recognize the love they must surely have felt but were afraid to reveal?

I don't know if we can fully appreciate the spot these parents were in. They knew that anyone who claimed Jesus was the Messiah was subject to excommunication from the synagogue (vs. 23). That terrified them; that punishment was a heavy one for the devout Jew. In the presence of what the parents knew would surely happen if they fell in line with their son, they fearfully responded by stating, "We know this is our son and that he was born blind, but we don't know what happened to make him see, or who did it. He is old enough to speak for himself. Ask him" (vs. 20).

REARRAIGNMENT OF THE MAN

So for the second time they called in the man who had been born blind and told him, "Give the glory to God, not to Jesus, for we know Jesus is an evil person" (vs. 24).

Cross-examination and intimidation. The man is beginning to see spiritually. Praise God for the work of grace in a man's heart when he takes his first few steps toward Jesus! He must be true to his own senses, and those senses told him that he was cured.

"I don't know whether he is good or bad," the man replied, "but I know this: *I was* blind, and now I see!"

Impatience on the part of the once-blind man now rears its head. He knew Jesus had worked a miracle; he is feeling something inside him that he never felt before.

"Look!" the man exclaimed. "I told you once; didn't you listen? Why do you want to hear it again? Do you want to become his disciples too?" (vs. 27).

Then they cursed him and said, "You are his disciple, but we are disciples of Moses. We know God has spoken to Moses, but as for this fellow, we don't know anything about him."

"Why that's very strange!" the man replied. "He can heal blind men, and yet you don't know anything about him! Well, God doesn't listen to evil men, but he has open ears to those who worship him and do his will. Since the

world began there has never been anyone who could open
the eyes of someone born blind. If this man were not
from God, he couldn't do it" (vss. 28–33).

Wearied, irritated, and provoked, the man preaches a
sermon that has echoed down through the centuries. I'm sure
he surprised even himself.

OUT, OUT, OUT!

"You illegitimate bastard, you!" they shouted. "Are you
trying to teach us?" And they threw him out (vs. 34).

They cut him off completely, and from that moment on he
had no right to cross the threshold of the Temple or synagogue.

Jesus will not leave us alone and comfortless in our hour
of trial; he can be counted on to help us pick up the pieces
of broken dreams and splintered hopes.

When Jesus heard what had happened, he found the man
and said, "Do you believe in the Messiah?"
The man answered, "Who is he, sir, for I want to."
"You have seen him," Jesus said, "and he is speaking
to you!"
"Yes, Lord," the man said, "I believe!" And he wor-
shiped Jesus.
Then Jesus told him, "I have come into the world to give
sight to those who are spiritually blind and to show those
who think they see that they are blind" (vss. 35–39).

I can find nothing more suitable with which to close this
chapter than the prayer of one called Jones of Nayland.
"Give us, O Lord, the sight of this man who had been blind
from birth, and deliver us from the blindness of his judges,
who had been learning all their lives, and yet knew nothing.
And if the world should cast us out, let us be found of Thee,
whom the world crucified." [1]

[1] J. C. Ryle, p. 618.

14

The Third and Fourth "I Am's":
Jesus, Tender Shepherd

The Text: John 10
The Place: Jerusalem
The Event: A Continuation of the Discourse with the
            Pharisees; Jesus Asserts His Divinity

There is no door so closed as the door to a closed mind and heart.

In the previous chapter we saw the once-blind man thrown out of the synagogue, but he finds heaven instead when he is found by Christ and chooses to let Christ into his heart's door. In *The Gospel According to John,* Morgan, quoting Bishop Westcott, says, "The separation between the old and the new was now consummated, when the rejected of the Jews sank prostrate at the feet of the Son of man." [1]

Now, once again, conscious of who his audience was, ever mindful of their background, Christ declares himself to be the Good Shepherd. It was an apt choice. His hearers should have understood immediately, for they were so familiar with the Old Testament, where passage after passage of Messianic Scriptures say that he will come to Israel as their Shepherd. Now, in fulfillment of these Scriptures, he stands humbly in their midst and declares that he is the Door and the Good Shepherd (John 10:1–6).

[1] G. Campbell Morgan, p. 171.

THE CLAIMS

While the picture Jesus presented to them in this parable was familiar, portraying as it did the shepherd function, yet its application was not understood.

> Then said Jesus unto them again, "Verily, verily, I say unto you, I am the door of the sheep. All that ever came before me are thieves and robbers: but the sheep did not hear them. I am the door: by me if any man enter in, he shall be saved, and shall go in and out, and find pasture. The thief cometh not, but for to steal, and to kill, and to destroy: I am come that they might have life, and that they might have it more abundantly" (vss. 7–10 AV).

Now their minds were beginning to grasp the hidden meaning in his words. The religious leaders had just thrown a man out of the door of the synagogue, out of their "fold." Jesus took him into another. The Door stands for the way of entrance, and the Shepherd represents the one who is in authority deciding who may enter. He came to redeem men from the curse of wrong human leadership and authority. The people were as perplexed and helpless wandering sheep. There was no safety nor protection in the fold of legalistic Pharisaism. Jesus did not wish to annihilate sinners; he came to find them, to lead them as a good shepherd and bring them into the safety and shelter of his care and love.

It is a beautiful portrait, full of tender meaning: Jesus pitting himself as a shepherd with a happy little lamb in his arms against the Pharisaic system with its domination and slavery.

Rivals of Christ in any age are robbers and thieves. Nothing is more opposite to true Christianity than the kind of hypocritical devotion these Pharisees displayed. With a grand stroke Jesus brushed the false leadership of the Pharisees away, declaring himself to be the Door into the sheepfold as well as the Shepherd. Plain directions were given as to how one may enter his sheepfold: through faith in him, as the great Mediator between God and man. Again, to the blind-hearted enemies of Christ, this was blasphemy. His claims were incredible and the crowd was divided into two factions: the one group following on to hear and believe more, their hostility gone; and the other more hostile than ever, with murder in their eyes and hearts.

Loving to Death, Leading by Life

There are some who struggle with the fact that Christ made himself to be both the Door and the Shepherd. For people outside the fold, he is the Door. To those within, he is the Good Shepherd. He is as a door shut, to keep out thieves and robbers, and as a door open for passage and communication. We have our admission into the flock of God through Christ, the Door.

The function of the shepherd is to lead his sheep in safe places where the grass is fresh and green, and other places where they can drink sweet water. As the day wears on and as the sun gets hotter, he leads the sheep to where they will be sheltered from the scorching sun. But he does the choosing for them, and he it is who brings them back safely to the sheepfold at night.

"I am the Good Shepherd. The Good Shepherd lays down his life for the sheep" (vs. 11).

When my faith is tested and I am tempted to complain, I remind myself that there are no insurmountable problems for my Shepherd. He has gone before; he has faced them all; he will work them out. My part is to follow. Life is not a track meet or a marathon race to test endurance. It is a moment by moment following in the footsteps of the Good Shepherd.

Stop straining. Stop worrying. Listen to the voice of the Shepherd:

"I am the Good Shepherd and know my own sheep, and
they know me" (vs. 14).

THE AUTHORITY

As he interpreted what he meant by this parable, Jesus
made superhuman claims revealing the scope of his purpose
in coming. He knew they were thinking in terms of how they
could kill him, and so he says:

> "The Father loves me because I lay down my life that I
> may have it back again. No one can kill me without my
> consent—I lay down my life voluntarily. For I have the right
> and power to lay it down when I want to and also the right
> and power to take it again. For the Father has given me this
> right" (vss. 17, 18).

Contrary to the best of merely human shepherds, Jesus is
here seen making the stupendous claim that he has power over
both life and death. An earthly shepherd might get killed
while in the line of duty, and that would be his earthly end;
but in foretelling of his death, Jesus states that death cannot
hold him.

CONTROVERSY!

As was to be expected, Jesus' words had the immediate
effect of producing more division among the ranks of the
Jewish leaders (vss. 20, 21). C. S. Lewis makes the observation that Jesus mainly produced three effects upon his listeners
—hatred, terror, and adoration. There was no trace of people
expressing mild approval.

We come back to the once-blind man. His act of worship
had opened the door for him to come to the Good Shepherd.
There were those who recognized the significance of what
had gone on and of Jesus' subsequent teaching. They, too,
then entered by the door of faith, which door is still open to
all who wish to enter.

15

The Seventh Sign:
"If Only . . ."

The Text: John 11:1–24
The Place: Bethany
The Event: Jesus' Encounter with Martha

Everyone wants to go to heaven, but no one wants to die. I have not forgotten the prayer of one of my children at a tender age: "Thank You, God, for not having us die yet." Death coming at any age is a robber. We do what we can to hold the Grim Reaper at bay. The well-beaten path of death and grief is one we like to avoid. Someone has said that death for the Christian is not a period but a comma in the story of life. The question is rightly asked: Is death a wall or a doorway?

Jesus stood at death's door and gave answers to questions like that. In John eleven we have proof and prophecy of the life, present and eternal, which Christ gives to all who put their trust in him. We may call it death, but Jesus has shown that this is but an incident in the course of an endless life.

Friendship with Jesus, while it does not protect us from human sorrows, does give assurance of sympathy and relief. We cannot always understand the purposes of God. We are not expected to. But one thing is certain for that person who has the friendship of Jesus—the result of these things will be some eternal good, some revealing of "the glory of God," if not immediately, then eventually according to the Father's timetable. Mary and Martha, two sisters who were Jesus' friends, had to learn this.

TROUBLE IN BETHANY

The sisters had a brother, Lazarus. Jesus was a frequent and welcome guest in the home of these three. These friends were important to him. Lazarus was sick.

> So the two sisters sent a message to Jesus telling him, "Sir, your good friend is very, very sick" (John 11:3).

Barnhouse gives the illustration of the old gentleman who, in times of trouble, would pray, "Lord, your property is in danger.'" In our times of need, it is not necessary to tell God what to do. He does not need direction from us. It is enough, like those holy sisters of Bethany, to simply pray, "Lord, he whom thou lovest is sick."

The message reached Jesus (vss. 4–11).

THE LEISURE OF PERFECT LOVE

One would think that Jesus, loving these friends in Bethany as much as he did, would have immediately rushed off to be with them. But such was not the case. He stayed two days longer in the same place where he was. John is very careful to declare that the love of Jesus for these three friends was that of a strong, intelligent affection based upon perfect understanding. John prefaces the entire narrative by emphasizing, "Now Jesus loved Martha, and her sister, and Lazarus" (vs. 5 AV). It was in the leisure of this perfect love that Jesus finally turned his face once again toward Judea, knowing full well what awaited him there.

We know the delay was intentional and for a purpose. We know too that the delay caused Martha and Mary great pain and anguish of heart. Hearts are broken at such times; there is darkness, intense sorrow, the agony of parting as we stand at the bedside of loved ones. Calvin says: "Let believers learn to suspend their desires, if God does not stretch out his hand to help as soon as they think necessity requires. Whatever may be his delays, he never sleeps, and never forgets his people."

MAN'S EXTREMITY, GOD'S OPPORTUNITY

I think of our friends whose daughter was taken by death in the early bloom of life, how their hearts were saddened. Yet, because of this, they turned their lives over to Christ, and only eternity will reveal the far-reaching effects of Brenda's death and her parents' subsequent desire to glorify Christ. "God 'invaded' our lives, as it were, through this experience," they testify, "but, we can only praise and thank him for it!" [1] How true it is that if we knew all the answers, we would not need faith.

DIVINE WAYS ARE INSCRUTABLE

When Jesus finally did relate his intention to go to Bethany, the disciples objected. Judea was hostile. Hadn't the religious leaders taken up stones to kill him on his last visit there! Calmly, Jesus asserts the fact that hostility can not touch him until his hour arrives. Jesus tells his disciples that Lazarus is sleeping.

> The disciples, thinking Jesus meant Lazarus was having a good night's rest, said, "That means he is getting better!" But Jesus meant Lazarus had died.
> Then he told them plainly, "Lazarus is dead. And for your sake, I am glad I wasn't there, for this will give you another opportunity to believe in me. Come, let's go to him" (vss. 12–15).

We have here Jesus' view of what we call death. In the

[1] Helen Kooiman, *Cameos, Women Fashioned by God* (Wheaton, Ill.: Tyndale House Publishers, 1968), p. 109.

presence of death, we shall see Jesus interpreting the meaning of a believer's dying.

Jesus does not say, "I am glad Lazarus is dead." The caring Jesus takes no pleasure in seeing those whom he loves going through suffering, weeping, and dying. Jesus did say, "I am glad for *your* sake . . ." God's dealings with us are always for the purpose that we might believe more, that we might trust him more, that there might be an increase of faith.

When they arrived at Bethany, they were told that Lazarus had already been in his tomb for four days. Bethany was only a couple miles down the road from Jerusalem, and many of the Jewish leaders had come to pay their respects and to console Martha and Mary on their loss. When Martha got word that Jesus was coming, she went to meet him. But Mary stayed at home. Martha said to Jesus, "Sir, if you had been here, my brother wouldn't have died. And even now it's not too late, for I know that God will bring my brother back to life again, if you will only ask him to."

Jesus told her, "Your brother will come back to life again."

"Yes," Martha said, "when everyone else does, on Resurrection Day" (vss. 17–24).

"IF ONLY . . ."

The long-looked-for one had come at last! Martha was the first to run and meet him. Varying interpretations are given to Martha's outburst. I find myself trying to imagine my own reaction. I am sure that throughout the ordeal of seeing my dearly-loved brother hovering between life and death, I would have folded my hands and lifted my eyes heavenward, crying out, "Oh God, if only Jesus were here!" Those words, "if only . . ." would have come from my lips many times.

So we hear Martha repeating in substance what I believe she had been saying all along. This was a natural expression of poignant grief.

Martha could have allowed the sorrow and disappointment in Jesus' failure to come on time to make her bitter. How many there are who do that—those who blame God for the death of loved ones or some other devastating personal experience, who feel God has failed them and consequently they refuse to have anything to do with him, with other Christians, or with the Church.

What Martha forgot in the anguish of the hour was that Jesus' presence was not needed to prevent Lazarus' death. There is wonderful consolation for us here. Our faith becomes entangled with unbelief; our emotions get in the way. We are not perfect angels nor saints without wings; we are at best converted sinners constantly standing in the need of God's mercy and grace.

Martha's characteristic temperament shows, but it is for our learning. Beware when you give release to your grief that you do not lose hold of your faith. There is such a thing as being so crushed and stunned by death, sickness, or some other traumatic experience, that we fail to conduct ourselves as those who believe God is always in control and that his will is being accomplished. Martha did evidence some faith, albeit a shaky sort of faith (vs. 22).

Mary stayed behind when Jesus sent word. She typifies the passive, silent, and meditative believer. Martha, in contrast, by rousing herself from her grief and stepping out with limited faith, heard Jesus make the glorious declaration about himself that has brought more comfort and hope to believers down through the centuries than any other words. The observation has been made that the well-ordered church must find room, place, and work for the Marys as well as the Marthas.

The Age-old Question

Martha, in a few words, poured out her heart to Jesus. What she hadn't said, he knew anyway. Yes, our wonderful caring Jesus knows when we are thinking, "Lord, it's too late, I don't understand. Does love let the beloved die? How our Lord must have inwardly hurt that day! Festo Kivengere, respected African evangelist, says there was smog in Bethany the day Jesus arrived. As far as the sisters were concerned the situation was hopeless. Martha was hoping desperately against hope that somehow things would be alright, but tears blurred her vision, and the future seemed dim and indistinct even after Jesus came.

Love to Christ, in Christian women, it has been said, is often much clearer than faith and knowledge. We are more prone to succumb to the emotional impact of a situation, rather than weighing the matter carefully and giving things time to work themselves out. We react with honest impulsiveness. But some events demand patience. Quiet waiting. In reflecting about those dark days in Bethany later on, both women would have had to agree that this was a supreme trial of their patience. I wish a Gospel According to Martha and Mary had been written; but there is none.

Martha wavered between near-despair and hopeful optimism; swaying between grief and a recognition that Jesus, in times past, has shown himself all-powerful. Martha did not fully understand the relationship between the Father and the Son. She spoke more out of love than adequate faith and knowledge.

When Jesus said to her, "Your brother shall rise again," he was predicting what was about to occur. It would seem, from Martha's reply, that she had a good understanding of the resurrection on the last day (vs. 24).

Present desolation often finds little or no comfort in the fact of a future resurrection of the dead. Martha was saying in her heart, "That's cold comfort, Jesus. It's a far distant event. That is little consolation right now." In our groaning and discontent under pressure of present crosses, we show the Martha-spirit. In her reply, Martha affirmed the faith she had, but in her spirit she failed to reflect the faith she claimed to possess. We are a paradox to ourselves and to the world, which is watching to see how we react under the stress of trial.

Can we learn that it is our relationship to Jesus, our ever-present help in time of trouble, that gives comfort and hope both for the life we live in the here and now and for the life that is to come in the hereafter? Martha at the time experienced temporary defeatism—everyone knows what that is like—while she was dead to the reality of the Hope of the world who stood before her. But death is not the final word! Believe it and move on with Jesus.

16

The Fifth "I Am":
Jesus at Death's Door

The Text: John 11:25–44
The Place: Bethany
The Event: Lazarus Raised to Life

We reach instinctively for the hand of Jesus when we are at death's door. As Christians, we know he understands and cares because we have his incomparable promise as spoken to Martha.

THE INCOMPARABLE PROMISE

"I am the resurrection, and the life; he that believeth in me, though he were dead (die), yet shall he live: And whosoever liveth and believeth in me shall never die. Believest thou this?" (John 11:25, 26 AV).

The question posed to Martha is one we can answer affirmatively. Those of us who have seen loved ones go through that door marked "death" will confidently say this is *the* great Christian declaration: *He that liveth and believeth on me (Jesus) shall never die.* That is the Christian's blessed hope. It has silenced the wisest of philosophers down through the centuries and given inexpressible hope and comfort to all who have stood in the place of mourning.

90

In the preceding chapter we looked at Martha, identifying with her in her sorrow, noting her weaknesses and yet that element of hope, which, though it flickered, was never quite extinguished. In the presence of Jesus, you can count on it, there will be answers to your questions as you lay them before him, and wait on him for a revelation of his love and care. If you are struggling right now, in the midst of some invisible inner war, where reason and emotion are clashing with some small degree of faith that you've managed to hold onto, my plea is this: Hand your doubts over to Jesus, let him clear away the debris of unbelief. Jesus stood at death's door—the tomb of Lazarus—and proved himself to be for all time the Comforter, the one who strengthens and sees us through. What he said to Martha, he is saying to you (vss. 25, 26).

THE AUTHOR OF RESURRECTION

Jesus told Martha that he was not only their teacher and friend, but that he was God, the Author of resurrection and the source of life, the one who holds the keys of death and the grave in his hands. He was telling her that if she believed in him only as a prophet sent to speak good and comfortable thing, she had then only received half the truth.

The sentence of death upon mankind came with original sin. We cannot get away from it—the effects of death are dismal and the bonds of death are strong; therefore, the urging to believe in Jesus while living is so vital. We do not die eternally; we can have a life that never ends; it comes, Jesus said, as a gift for believing in him. The sting of bodily death is taken away. Death, for that one who entrusts himself in life to Jesus, then becomes a threshhold ushering him into the presence of Jesus. Heaven and Jesus await the believer as he passes through death's door. His soul lives on uninterruptedly forevermore. This is the promise of blessed immortality. What was begun as weak faith in this life, is perfected in eternal life.

But there is even more! The body shall not be forever dead in the grave. Jesus said he is the One who raises the dead, and they shall have a glorious resurrected body.

When Jesus asked Martha if she believed what he had to say, she answered: "Yes, Master. I believe you are the Messiah, the Son of God, the one we have so long awaited" (vs. 27). Pressed for an answer, Martha, even while in the confusion that accompanies grief, gives a good confession of her faith in Christ. Faith has been defined as an echo to divine revelation. Light has been shed; Martha stood in its brilliant rays and displayed the marvelous grace of our loving Lord.

To pause and recognize this fifth great "I am" of Jesus is in order. The devout Jew would be familiar with God's great utterance to Moses at the time God commissioned him to lead the children of Israel out of Egyptian bondage. Moses questioned God: "What shall I say to the people when they ask who you are and what is your name?" (Ex. 3:13). The magnificent, awe-inspiring word came back from God: "I AM THAT I AM: Thus shalt thou say unto the children of Israel, I AM hath sent me unto you" (vs. 14). This was the Sovereign God, the God of their ancestors speaking. Whether or not this thought flashed through Martha's mind we do not know. But, as a devout Jewess, schooled in the rich Jewish tradition, she would under normal circumstances react to the use of the words I AM. I personally believe that hearing Jesus say, "I AM the resurrection and the life . . ." put new life and hope back into Martha. She sprung into action; no more was she immoble, paralyzed by grief, but she responded at once by leaving Jesus to go get her sister.

CHRIST CALLS FOR MARY

Jesus had just said to her (in effect), "I AM all that is necessary for the present difficult situation, and I AM all that you need for the unknown future," and with that word ringing in her ears she calls her sister aside from the mourners.

"Jesus is here and wants to see you." So Mary went to him at once. . . . When the Jewish leaders who were at the house trying to console Mary saw her leave so hastily, they assumed she was going to Lazarus' tomb to weep; so they followed her.

When Mary arrived where Jesus was, she fell down at his feet, saying, "Sir, if you had been here, my brother would still be alive."

When Jesus saw her weeping and the Jewish leaders wailing with her, he was moved with indignation and deeply troubled. "Where is he buried?" he asked them. They told him, "Come and see" (vss. 28–34).

Morgan makes the observation that to Martha Jesus gave his teaching and the promise of life; to Mary, quiet even in the midst of sorrow, he gave his tears and the activity of life, thus revealing to her the cost to himself of the victory to be won.[1]

The Posture of Submissive Sorrow

Matthew Henry calls attention to Mary's posture. She fell at Jesus' feet, as one overwhelmed with a passionate sorrow. She fell down as a sinking mourner and as a humble petitioner. Humility and submissiveness are always good Christian graces. "She fell at his feet, as one submitting to his will in what was done, and referring herself to his good-will in what was now to be done." [2]

While Mary uttered the same words as Martha, we are led to believe there was a different intonation, another emphasis. "This is proved by the effect produced upon the Lord, for his method is ever that of replying to what the condition demands. Martha's agonized perplexity called for teaching. Mary's surging but submissive sorrow asked for sympathy, and this was supplied by an unveiling to her of his own sorrow." [3]

We have seen Mary before at Jesus' feet in an attitude of adoration and discipleship. Then all was well and Lazarus was

[1] G. Campbell Morgan, *The Analysed Bible*, p. 158.
[2] *Matthew Henry's Commentary, Vol. V* (Old Tappan, N.J.: Fleming H. Revell Co., n.d.), p. 1053.
[3] Morgan, p. 158.

alive. On that occasion Martha tried to express her love for Jesus in service and busy activity. She ended up grumbling at her sister and criticizing Jesus. "Now when the clouds had blotted out the sunshine, when sorrow had come, and Mary's heart was breaking, she went back to the same place, back to Jesus' feet." [4]

This is a very emotional scene. Mary was devastated. Such will always be the reaction of those who mourn: either they will evidence self-control such as Martha did, or the intensity of grief will so overwhelm them that they abandon themselves to the instinctive reaction of the moment. Jesus showed no displeasure with either woman.

THE SYMPATHY OF JESUS

Jesus' sympathies were always quick and keen. He, too, was a man of intense emotions. There was a mixture of indignation and sorrow. Why anger? Jesus was concentrating his attention upon sin, as the underlying cause of all suffering, grief, and sorrow. He was filled with indignation against sin. We see the mingling of pain and anger; anger at the cause, pain in the presence of the effect. Jesus groaned within; this was no counterfeit sympathy designed to impress the onlookers, many of whom were likewise mourning. The idea expressed is one of deep sighing. Isaiah the prophet tells us that in all our afflictions God is afflicted. When we truly love our friends, we will share with them in their griefs as well as their joys. Friendship is communication of affection. Jesus is the Friend of those who mourn.

Chafed in spirit, deeply troubled, Jesus took into his own heart all the agony, all the misery resulting from sin, represented in a dead man—his friend Lazarus—and the broken-hearted people around him. It is at this point in the narrative that we have that profound verse in the Bible, the shortest actually, but one heavy with meaning:

Jesus wept (vs. 35 AV).

[4] G. Campbell Morgan, *The Gospel According to John*, p. 196.

We have here further proof of Jesus' true humanity; he was not only absolutely divine but also truly human. He fully entered into fellowship with the sorrow of the moment. Isaiah the prophet foretold that he was to be a man of sorrows and acquainted with grief (Isa. 53:3).

> The sickness and death of Lazarus, is still down through the centuries, like the expanding circle on the water when a stone has fallen into the pool. The fact that this man grew sick and died comes to you today to tell you that your sicknesses and your catastrophes are not too great; that you are in the hands of the Savior; that nothing has ever touched you that has not passed through his will; that he wants you as you are for his honor and his glory; that he is able to take care of that situation in your home; that he is able to give you triumph in a body that is crippled or that is diseased or that is losing some of its faculties; that he knows what he's doing. He's with you in your loneliness. He knows all about it. Let the ripples of Lazarus' experience wash the shores of your life today.
>
> And as you go on in life, you can go with a renewed certainty in the sovereignty of God that he doeth all things well, that nothing has ever come to you that wasn't tailor-made and measured to fit your exact circumstances and your exact need. Our Lord is on the throne! [5]

Do not make the mistake of giving a limited interpretation to those tears of Jesus, as the Jews did that day. Some of them said, "This fellow healed a blind man, why couldn't he keep Lazarus from dying?" The response of Jesus to this comment was one of anger (vs. 38).

Yes, of course Jesus could have prevented Lazarus' dying. His power was unlimited. But we do not have here a question of power; it is one of purpose. God, in this instance, limited himself by his own purpose.

The weeping of Christ can be instructive. Jesus entered into the grief of his friends; repression was not his way. It is no sin to sorrow; you need not be ashamed of deep feelings

[5] Donald Grey Barnhouse, pp. 148, 149.

that move you to tears. To be cold and stoical is no sign of special grace. Tears are a gift of God. They are for our benefit; they give release to that deep inner pain that is so real. We feel bereft. We are not unfeeling robots. Cry. It is normal. It is perfectly natural. It is right. Jesus in the presence of death did not stand back in icy detachment. God shares in our sorrows. Draw comfort from the fact that Jesus is as able to feel as he is able to save.

JESUS AT THE TOMB

The crucial moment has now come.

> Then they came to the tomb. It was a cave with a heavy stone rolled across its door. "Roll the stone aside," Jesus told them. But Martha said, "By now the smell will be terrible, for he has been dead four days." "But didn't I tell you that you will see a wonderful miracle from God if you believe?" Jesus asked her.
>
> So they rolled the stone aside. Then Jesus looked up to heaven and said, "Father, thank you for hearing me. (You always hear me, of course, but I said it because of all these people standing here, so that they will believe you sent me.)" Then he shouted, "Lazarus, come out!"
>
> And Lazarus came—bound up in the gravecloth, his face muffled in a head swath. Jesus told them, "Unwrap him and let him go!" (vss. 38–44).

CHRIST, CONQUEROR OF DEATH

As we retrace those momentous happenings, we see Martha shrinking back, fear etched all over her face. Martha's faith broke down at the last minute. The laws of death would dictate that disintegrative processes were well started in the body of her brother. Jesus silenced her with a gentle reproof meant to reinforce her faith in him. Love linked with omnipotence, and Lazarus came forth. A corpse already corrupt was made alive!

As the crowd looked on with breathless expectation, Jesus

prayed audibly to the Father and the mighty miracle took place. Christ proved himself to be Conqueror of death. With beautiful delicacy, John draws a veil over the effect of all of this on Martha and Mary.

There is much comfort here. No one is too far gone in sin for Christ to raise up to newness of life in the here and now. He is as mighty to save and restore sinful humans as he was to raise a dead man.

When we lie down in the grave, we have the full assurance that we shall rise again. If Jesus had not prefaced "Come forth" with Lazarus' name, every grave on the face of the earth that day would have opened. Such is the power of Jesus.

17

Sequels of the Lazarus Miracle: Love Cares Without Computing

The Text: John 11:45–57; 12:1–8
The Place: Jerusalem; Ephraim; Bethany
The Event: The Cabal Conspiring to Kill Jesus; Jesus and His Disciples Withdraw; The Supper at Bethany Shortly Before the Passover

Love cannot afford to be anything but lavish. Lavish in its bestowal on the object of its love. Even extravagant. It has nothing whatsoever to do with money. Dollars-and-cents value is not the criterion by which love is to be evaluated. In the final analysis it costs nothing to lavishly give love; yet, it can cost everything. We say we love, but we prove it when we put content into our words. In the concluding verses of John 11 and the first seven verses of John 12 we observe love in action and the consequences of such unstinting giving.

While Jesus' shout calling Lazarus forth from the grave brought life to this much-loved friend, the crowd's shout, we shall see, in subsequent chapters, brought death to Jesus. The miracle of love only increased Jesus' enemies fear of him and resulted in further efforts on their part to plot his death. But it also had the effect of giving new life—spiritual birth—to "many of the Jewish leaders who were with Mary and saw it happen, and finally believed on him" (John 11:45).

THE COURSE OF EXPEDIENCY

In his tabulation of results John tells us that those who did not come to believe on him "went away to the Pharisees and reported it [the bringing of Lazarus back to life] to them" (vs. 46).

> Then the chief priests and Pharisees convened a council to discuss the situation.
> "What are we going to do?" they asked each other. "For this man certainly does miracles. If we let him alone the whole nation will follow him—and then the Roman army will come and kill us and take over the Jewish government" (vss. 47, 48).

It was a coalition between the chief priests (Sadducees) and the Pharisees. The Sadducees were in diametric opposition in philosophy and religion to the beliefs of the Pharisees. They were as coals to burning coals and wood to fire in their mutual irritation of this one called Jesus, and they heaped their enmity, rage, and fear together, inflaming one another still more.

Their logic was cunning but vile. Under the guise of patriotism, with elegant phraseology, they would seduce the people's thinking. Political expediency and national well-being were at stake. Yes, that would be their tack. It is not difficult to picture these conniving council members stroking their beards as they plotted their diabolical course of action.

I cannot imagine winning a popularity contest or holding an audience for long by standing up and stating: "You know nothing at all!" Yet, Caiaphas, the High Priest, got away with it. But God used this thoroughly bad man, this implacable enemy of his Son, to make an unconscious prophecy full of light and truth. The speech Caiaphas made was contemptuous and cruel. It was dark with sin and evil intent. But in the extraordinary direction of Heaven the mouths of wicked men can utter truth, contrary to their own intentions, which God will use for his design and purpose.

COLD-BLOODED DYNAMISM

Caiaphas . . . declared, "You know nothing at all. Nor do you understand *or* reason out that it is expedient *and* better for your own welfare that one man should die on behalf of the people than that the whole nation should perish (be destroyed, ruined)."

Now he did not say this simply of his own accord—he was not self-moved; but being the high priest that year, he prophesied that Jesus was to die for the nation (Isa. 53:8).

And not only for the nation, but also for the purpose of uniting into one body the children of God who have been scattered far and wide (Isa. 49:6) (vss. 49–52 *The Amplified Bible*).

Caiaphas was being politically sagacious. Chalk this up as the most dastardly political speech on record. The philosophy of this man finds its counterpart among some politicians today.

THE CRUEL CONSPIRACY BEGINS IN EARNEST

So from that time on the Jewish leaders began plotting Jesus' death (vs. 53).

In the presence of those who had lost their capacity for caring, who were held in the tenacious grip of self-will and sin, "Jesus now stopped his public ministry and left Jerusalem; he went to the edge of the desert, to the village of Ephraim, and stayed there with his disciples" (vs. 54).

QUIETNESS BEFORE THE STORM

In the economy of God Jesus withdrew until his hour came. The shadows of the cross were already falling across the path of the Word who became Man. He needed a period of quietness with his disciples before the storm broke.

The Passover, a Jewish holy day, was near, and many country people arrived in Jerusalem several days early so that they could go through the cleansing ceremony before the Passover began. They wanted to see Jesus, and as they gossiped in the Temple, they asked each other, "What do you think? Will he come for the Passover?"

Meanwhile the chief priests and Pharisees had publicly announced that anyone seeing Jesus must report him immediately so that they could arrest him" (vss. 55–57).

Unquestionably, Jesus was *the* man of the hour. The Jerusalem Jews were out to get Jesus. If Jesus was true to form, then the pilgrims arriving in Jerusalem and the residents of the city itself could anticipate with reasonable certainty that he would put in an appearance. Gossipmongers flourished in Jesus' day also. Talk is cheap. Jesus had been labeled as a traitor to the "church" and the nation. Would the edict against him keep him away? The people wondered and talked.

HONOR EVEN IN THE DEPTHS OF HUMILIATION

Six days before the Passover ceremonies began, Jesus arrived in Bethany. . . . A banquet was prepared in Jesus' honor. Martha served, and Lazarus sat at the table with him. Then Mary took a jar of costly perfume made from essence of nard, and anointed Jesus' feet with it and wiped them with her hair. And the house was filled with fragrance (John 12:1–3).

This was the fragrance of love; more than the sweet aroma of the anointment was the act of the anointing. Yes, Martha, we would expect to find you serving; and yes, Mary, we are not surprised to find you once more at the feet of Jesus.

I, however, cannot find it in my heart to criticize Martha. (Someone has to do the so-called "dirty work," the menial tasks, if the rest are to enjoy themselves.) Martha had learned her lesson well on a previous occasion when Jesus was a guest at dinner; this time we do not hear her complaining. Jesus *is* the very best Teacher. When he reproves, it is for our own good. When we stoop to service in any capacity where Christ may be honored, there is a fragrance there, too, that will not be overlooked by Jesus. Modern Marthas do not need to take a back seat to the Marys; Martha's serving was not without significance.

Surely many at the banquet must have known that a crisis was at hand. In the presence of joyful hospitality there must have been an undercurrent of apprehension; the notices that were out concerning Jesus must have reached the ears of these his friends. I cannot help but wonder what thoughts cycled through the mind of Lazarus as he sat at the table with Jesus and the other guests. Lazarus in fellowship with Jesus says to me that while I was once dead in my sin, I, too, stand in that place of highest privilege where I can have blessed fellowship with Christ. But the atmosphere was one of happiness, comradeship, and quiet devotion. Jesus, knowing full well what terrible experiences lay ahead, did not let it disturb his composure. I am sure the eyes of everyone frequently turned to look at Lazarus—Lazarus just back from the grave, but unchanged, poised, and happy. What a joy-filled evening that must have been!

It is the radiant loveliness of Mary's action, however, that John focuses upon. He places her spontaneous act of love in stark contrast with the reaction of Judas.

There is much to be learned from Mary. In the days of sunshine we saw her sitting at the feet of Jesus. Quietness, discipleship, and adoration.

In the days of darkness, when her heart was broken, she went straight to his feet.

Now, in the day of *his* approaching darkness and sorrow, again she falls at his feet.

The scene deserves careful study. Because Jesus left for Ephraim after the raising of Lazarus, I am led to believe that this was the first time the Bethany family saw him after that mighty demonstration of his heaven-sent power. All three of them felt a deep sense of gratitude to Jesus for what he had done, but Mary, with that special sensitivity that characterized her whole outlook on life, longed for some means to communicate her true feelings. How could she possibly thank him enough?

There was more to it than that, however. The whole countryside was buzzing with rumors about Jesus; Mary had not shut her ears or her heart to these words of impending doom. Others listened also, but they did not hear or understand like the intuitive Mary. (Many women possess this unusual gift of intuitiveness; Mary is our spiritual antecedent.) There were many who were saying that Jesus had evaded his enemies before, slipping through the nooses they had laid for him, avoiding their stone-throwing, and if he could do it before, he'd do it again. Mary comprehended what the others did not: Jesus was going to die soon.

MARY'S THANK OFFERING

Mary acted on her feelings—an act of pure, passionate devotion animated by love. Her motive was strong: nothing was too good or too great to do for Jesus. This was the highest honour she could bestow upon him. This was the expression of her heart's adoration, and that is what all true worship really is.

William P. Barker explains the monetary value of the ointment that Mary so lavishly poured upon Jesus:

> Mary's little jar contained pure, undiluted ointment—the most expensive kind. Even the jar carved from alabaster, required a considerable outlay. Jar and contents were fantastically high-priced, costing three hundred denarii. One denarius equalled a good day's pay for an average working man; therefore, Mary's alabaster jar and ointment represented an investment of a man's total wages for about one year.
>
> Nearly all of Mary's life-savings were tied up in that jar. Because it was the high-priced stuff, she was obviously saving it for her own burial-anointing. A decent funeral with proper anointing was not an extravagance but a matter of propriety.[1]

I wonder if we can fathom the prodigality of her act and gift. This was not purposeless waste, but lavishness the likes of which no one in that room had ever seen before. She was

---

[1] William P. Barker, *Women and the Liberator* (Old Tappan, N.J.: Fleming H. Revell Co., 1972), pp. 95, 96.

exuberant and unrestrained as she threw caution away. She could not wait for the perfume to come out drop by drop, but breaks the beautiful bottle so its contents can pour over the feet of her beloved Master!

THE SMOKE SCREEN OF GUILT

We are not told the reaction of the guests, with the exception of that of Judas—and that is a notable exception.

> But Judas Iscariot, one of his disciples—the one who would betray him—said, "That perfume was worth a fortune. It should have been sold and the money given to the poor." Not that he (Judas) cared for the poor, but he was in charge of the disciples' funds and often dipped into them for his own use! (vss. 4–6).

Pilfering from the collection plate may have originated with Judas!

Covetousness is a dreadful sin. While Mary's act is one of the most beautiful acts of love that the entire Bible records, Judas' words stand out as being the mark of a selfish, loveless, joyless, greedy betrayer.

Would he really have taken Mary's exquisite gift and sold it and donated the proceeds to the poor!

Martha's expenditure on food was no small item, but Judas didn't mention that. (I wonder if he was stout; at any rate, I'm sure he enjoyed Martha's gift. Gluttony may also have been one of his vices; it would come as no surprise.)

Did the other guests release an audible, "Ohhhh . . ." as Mary wiped his feet with her beautiful hair? Was anyone besides Judas thinking how clumsy and wasteful: if so, were they mentally clicking off the mathematical equivalent of her love-gift? Judas' world was wallet-sized.

JESUS' STAMP OF APPROVAL

Jesus was not condoning waste and carelessness in his reply to Judas as he told him to shape up. The cruel avarice of this thief shows in the glaring light of the Light of the world as Jesus said:

"Let her alone. She did it in preparation for my burial. You can always help the poor, but I won't be with you very long" (vss. 7, 8).

Jesus was quick to rise to Mary's defense. That is worth remembering. When you are the victim of some supposedly noble-minded person's tongue and your spirit is crushed, rest assured that Jesus is jealously guarding his own. Consider the source of criticism when it is leveled at you; make certain you are in right standing with the Lord and your motives above suspicion; and then, carry on. Do not let your zeal for Jesus in any way be affected by the likes of a Judas.

"Jesus forever vindicates the most extravagant gifts which are made in devotion to him, and condemns the spurious philanthropy which is not animated by love for him. . . . Social service divorced from Christianity may spend the treasure of Mary according to the direction of Judas." [2]

Jesus was saying, in effect, to Judas and every other guest in that home, "Get your priorities in order. Charity is not necessarily the best way to help the poor: it is far better to give of yourself." Jesus put his stamp of approval on personal devotion to himself as our number one priority. You will never be impoverished by that gift that is bestowed upon the Son of God.

"Jesus' vibrations of caring for others prompted Mary to grab whatever was at hand to show her love." [3] That which is done in the spirit of Mary's impulsive and generous care is not for others to condemn. Ecclesiastes 7:1 says: "A good name smells sweeter than the finest ointment." Mary's good name carries with it the pleasant aroma of lavish, unconstrained caring.

"The fragrance of a good perfume spreads from the bed-

[2] Charles R. Erdman, p. 110.
[3] William P. Barker, p. 98.

room to the dining room; so does a good name spread from one end of the world to the other" (The Midrash Rabbah on Ecclesiastes 7:1).

Let us stand back in respectful awe and look at this lovely woman and her lavish love. Love cares without computing. May each of us have that "break the alabaster jar and pour it all out" type of love that cares as Jesus cares.

18

The Close of His Public Ministry:
A King on a Donkey?

The Text: John 12:9–50
The Place: Jerusalem
The Event: The Triumphal Entry

Jesus' earthly life was a demonstration that God is to be both the subject and the object of glory. To this end he lived and died.

THE GREAT PAGEANT

The great multitude who had come to the feast, when they heard that Jesus was coming to Jerusalem, took the branches of palm trees, and went out to meet him, and began to cry out, "Hosanna: BLESSED IS HE WHO COMES IN THE NAME OF THE LORD, even the King of Israel."

And Jesus, finding a young donkey, sat on it; as it is written, "FEAR NOT, DAUGHTER OF ZION: BEHOLD, YOUR KING COMES SITTING ON A DONKEY'S COLT" (John 12:12–15 NAS [capitals in text]).

This remarkable entry into Jerusalem caused the eyes of all Israel to be fixed upon Jesus. It must have been a tremendous audience, for the Pharisees with indignation and envy turned to each other and exclaimed, "Look—the whole world has gone after him!" (vs. 19).

Step by step, Jesus moved in perfect harmony with the Father's plan. Five hundred years before, the prophet Zechariah had foretold that the King of Zion would one day appear "riding upon an ass." Certainly this is not the way kings ordinarily travel! We associate great pomp and splendor with kings and their retinue. Kings were known to come with swords in their hand like conquerors, with powerful forces to back them up. Jesus came, however, not as a warrior, but as a peaceful, just, and holy King. No one watching this strange procession could spread the rumor that he came intending to wrest the kingdom of Judea out of the hand of the Romans or to drive Pontius Pilate and his legions out of the city!

Palm branches have always been an emblem of victory and triumph. The crowd waved the branches as an expression of joy. Someone started to chant "Hosanna: Blessed is he that cometh in the name of the Lord," and the multitude took up the refrain. In their acclamation they acknowledged him to be the long-expected Messiah. Of a certainty, many in that crowd knew what they were shouting and believed this; but others went along with the enthusiasm of the multitude, a fickle throng swayed by low motives, wanting him to satisfy their earthly expectations and set up the "Kingdom of their father David." It has been said that the voices which that day cried, "Hosanna," very soon after hissed, "Crucify." We have no way of knowing how many forsook the one they were now proclaiming as king.

PROPHECY BEING FULFILLED, THEN AND NOW

John, in writing about this later, made an interesting confession:

> (His disciples didn't realize at the time that this was a fulfillment of prophecy; but after Jesus returned to his glory in heaven, then they noticed how many prophecies of Scripture had come true before their eyes.) (vs. 16).

They were unconscious actors in the mightiest drama of all time. That day Jesus moved quietly on. As he looked at the crowd and beheld the city, he wept over it (Luke 19:41). A King crying? His eye (seeing) affected his heart, and his heart his eye again. This was a triumphal entry, yet he wept.

REPRESENTATIVES OF THE WORLD AT LARGE

John relates the arrival of some Greeks to worship at the feast and their subsequent inquiry of Philip as to the possibility of seeing Jesus (vss. 21, 22).

The presence of those Greeks drew from the lips of Jesus these words:

> "Truly, truly, I say to you, unless a grain of wheat falls into the earth and dies, it remains by itself alone; but if it dies, it bears much fruit.
> "He who loves his life loses it; and he who hates his life in this world shall keep it to life eternal.
> "If any one serves me, let him follow me; and where I am, there shall my servant also be; if any one serves me, the Father will honor him" (vss. 24–26 NAS).

Jesus prefaced those words by calling himself *Son of Man.* He was altogether unique among men; only he could make that claim for himself. This is certainly a keynote statement of our Lord. All along he has been alluding to "the hour." Now the approach of these Greeks from outside the Jewish covenant is prophetic to Jesus of the gathering to him of peoples of all nations and tongues. The title *Son of Man* links him to the whole human family, and he answers his disciples by saying:

> "The hour has come for the Son of Man to be glorified" (vs. 23 NAS).

WHAT PRICE GLORY?

The hour? What hour? Glory? What kind of glory? Did those thoughts rush through the disciples' minds? Jesus stood in the midst of wickedness, the apostasy in Israel was complete, and as he looked at that shocking landscape representative of the human spirit and of human history, he knew the hour was at hand.

Have you ever held a tiny seed of grain in your hand? There isn't much to see, is there? But drop it into the earth; wait and watch a few days. Soon there is a small green sprout pushing its way up through the soil, first the blade, then in time the ear, and then a full ear of corn. All of that was in that one tiny grain, though you could not see it. But that isn't all. Husk that ear, take out all the grains, put them back into the ground, and watch and wait some more.

Seed must be put into the ground, must decay and die, if we want it to bear fruit and produce a crop. You can never reap a harvest by hoarding the seed, refusing to bury it. Christ was the immortal seed. He had to go down into death, lie in the grave like seed under the clods; but as seed comes up green, fresh, flourishing, and with a greater increase, so Jesus would emerge from death, producing a rich, spiritual harvest that would go on and on. Only through Christ's death would a mighty harvest spring up for the benefit of all mankind.

Each of us in whom the life of Christ lives, are as seeds. We have a spark of Jesus' life in us, but that germ of life is so often surrounded by our own selfish desires. But when we dare to die to self and point all our desires on the glory of God and the outworking of his perfect will in our lives, then fruit is inevitable. What we need to do is to be willing to die.

Did the disciples that day catch something of what Jesus was saying? Jesus had spoken of being glorified. Somber glory, to be sure, lay ahead. But the glory of the cross would illumine the world from that day to this.

> "If any one serves me, let him follow me; and where I am, there shall my servant also be; if any one serves me, the Father will honor him" (vs. 26 NAS).

THE SON IS TROUBLED AND HEAVEN ANSWERS

"Now my soul is deeply troubled. Shall I pray, 'Father, save me from what lies ahead'? But that is the very reason why I came! Father, bring glory and honor to your name" (vss. 27, 28).

Jesus troubled? The Son of Man, the Savior of the world, God incarnate troubled? He who could heal diseases with a mere touch, give sight to the blind, command even the winds and the waves to obey him, in deep distress, in great agony and conflict of spirit?

Jesus was feeling the burden of man's sin pressing down upon him. This was the mighty weight of the world's guilt imputed to him. The sin of our soul was the trouble of Christ's soul; the trouble of his soul was designed to ease the trouble of our souls. Later we shall hear him say, "Let not your heart be troubled." Why should yours and mine be troubled when he has already troubled himself for us?

Jesus submitted to trouble in his soul; it was holy mourning, the prelude to the eternal joy he was prepared to secure for us through the way of voluntary humiliation and suffering. But even while (in his true humanity, in the height of anguish) he cries out, he checks himself in beautiful acquiescence to the Father's will, and quickly adds: "But for this purpose I came to this hour."

God in heaven could not keep silence; Heaven answered the Son's prayer with an articulate voice:

> "I have already done this [glorified the Father's name], and
> I will do it again" (vs. 28b).

The name of God had been glorified in the life of Christ— in his miracles, the doctrine he gave, the lessons he taught, his example of holiness and goodness, the love he showed, the ways he cared—but that name above all names would be further glorified in Jesus' death. This was the third time in the course of Jesus' earthly life that heaven broke silence.

JESUS ANNOUNCES THE CRISIS POINT IN HUMAN HISTORY

While the opinion of the bystanders concerning this voice was varied (vs. 29), on one thing they were agreed—something uncommon had definitely happened; an extraordinary noise had been heard. Words or thunder, it was for real.

> Then Jesus told them, "The voice was for your benefit, not mine. The time of judgment for the world has come—and the time when Satan, the prince of this world, shall be cast out. And when I am lifted up (on the cross), I will draw everyone to me." He said this to indicate how he was going to die (vss. 30–33).

Judgment? Did that word penetrate their thinking? Who wants to be judged? Judgment hints at a verdict pending— either there is favor or condemnation, pardon or sentencing. The people were puzzled. The prediction of his death was offensive. (The offense of the cross has not ceased.) Guilty men are still troubled by the truth relative to a crucified Savior.

How can an enemy be overcome by a man hanging from a cross? They could not understand that Christ signed Satan's death warrant with his own blood. The cross is bloody, indelicate, crude, and nauseating. (I agree with Barnhouse's description.) At Christ's death the world-famous trial between Christ and Satan took place. From the vantage point of the world, Christ lost; but in the courts of heaven Christ is adjudged victorious over death and the grave. The grave in the final analysis could not hold him, the fallen seed burst forth into life, triumphant over death and the enemy.

Notice the reaction of the crowd:

> "Die?" asked the crowd. "We understood that the Messiah would live forever and never die. What Messiah are you talking about?" (vs. 34).
>
> Jesus ignored their theological problem, and said: "My light will shine out for you just a little while longer. Walk in it while you can, and go where you want to go before the darkness falls, for then it will be too late for you to find your way. Make use of the Light while there is still time, then you will become light bearers."
>
> After saying these things, Jesus went away and was hidden from them (vss. 34–36).

THE CONDEMNATION OF UNBELIEF

But despite all the miracles he had done, most of the people would not believe he was the Messiah (vss. 37–43). Their consciences were so hardened and seared that they lost the will to believe, consequently they had no power. It was the fault of the human will, not that of God that they *would* not believe. God does not will the death of any sinner; but through continued hardened impenetance and an unwillingness to come to terms with the truth of the cross, a person may provoke God to give them up (vss. 44–50).

PART III

Private Ministry to His Disciples

19

The Ministry of Love:
Christ the Servant

The Text: John 13
The Place: The Last Supper in the Upper Room in Jerusa-
             lem
The Event: Jesus Sums Up His Claims: He Washes the
             Disciples' Feet and Gives Them a New Com-
             mandment

The caring Jesus was always motivated by perfect, unfailing
love. Before he stooped to the death of the cross (a more
ignominious way of dying can scarcely be imagined), he con-
descended to do something else in an act of complete self-
forgetfulness, mindful only of the needs of his disciples. The
memorable act of washing the dirty feet of the disciples was
to be a picture of the voluntary humiliation whereby he laid
aside his rights and took the lowly place of a servant. This
sublime act did more than cleanse dirty feet; it cleansed their
hearts. Now they were prepared to receive his teaching.

> Now before the feast of the Passover, Jesus knowing that
> his hour had come that he should depart out of this world
> to the Father, having loved his own who were in the world,
> he loved them to the end (John 13:1 NAS).

THE SUPREME REVELATION OF LOVE

The depth and intensity of Jesus' love we cannot fully grasp.
Inside, I think, he was full of tears. He was going to leave

them; his public ministry had ended, and now, in this brief time together, he wanted to convey to this inner circle how much he loved them. There still remained much that he wanted to teach them as well.

As he looked at the faces of these twelve, his eyes traveled to their feet. It was customary in the home of the rich for a servant to wash the guests' feet. In that country where men traveled mostly by foot, their feet understandably got sweaty and dusty. In a company of men such as this, where there was no slave provided by the host to perform this task, it went undone, unless the one considered to be the lowest was asked to do it.

Jesus had perfect knowledge of all things. That meant that he knew Judas was about to betray him, and he also knew that his disciples would forsake him shamefully in a few hours (out of fear), but even so, he loved them to the last (vss. 2, 3). Christ's is a steadfast love that is not diminished even when we are so undeserving of it.

The strident voices of his enemies could not be heard in this quiet place; the hubbub of the curious crowd was still; he was alone with his own:

> So he got up from the supper table, took off his robe, wrapped a towel around his loins, poured water into a basin, and began to wash the disciples' feet and to wipe them with the towel he had around him (vss. 4, 5).

The towel girt about the loins in the East was the badge of slavery. What humility! John never forgot it; neither did Peter. "Gird yourselves with humility," this big fisherman wrote decades afterward as he remembered it all.

Would you have gotten squeamish at the thought of washing twelve pair of dirty feet at mealtime? But Christ did it! He who was equal with God, rose from the table and laid aside his glory and took upon himself the form of a servant, thereby teaching his followers that "he came not to be ministered to, but to minister." It was a symbolic unveiling of the great truth that we must come to Jesus to be cleansed from the guilt and stain of sin; we need daily cleansing from daily defilement.

A NOTABLE DIALOGUE

When he came to Simon Peter, Peter said to him, "Master, you shouldn't be washing our feet like this!" (vs. 6).

Peter, who was seldom at a loss for words, was so startled that, in amazement, he protested, *"Thou* washing *my* feet!" (italics author's.)

Jesus replied, "You don't understand now why I am doing it; some day you will" (vs. 7).

The idea of the Master washing his dirty feet was totally abhorrent and Peter drew his feet back, tucking them under his long robe.

"No," Peter protested, "you shall never wash my feet!"

Jesus was equally emphatic:

"But if I don't, you can't be my partner."

Simon Peter exclaimed,

"Then wash my hands and head as well—not just my feet!" (vss. 8, 9).

Then Jesus tenderly corrected Peter and explained for the benefit of all (vss. 10, 11). Jesus would not have us reject his offers of grace; Peter was not to make himself wiser than Jesus and dispute Jesus' command. Quickly Peter recovers. Those who have the love of Jesus within have no difficulty admitting error. Jesus is always ready to stoop and give of himself to that one who acknowledges his need for cleansing

THE APPLICATION

What Christ had done was to give an instructive sign. If we are to touch the world for Jesus it will be through loving as Jesus loved; it means doing whatever we can to ensure the happiness and well-being of others; we must lessen the sorrows of others and multiply their joys. Humility and love are two Christian graces that everyone understands and responds to. This, Jesus said, is *the* path of blessing (vss. 12–20).

JESUS FORETELLS HIS BETRAYER

Now Jesus was in great anguish of spirit and exclaimed, "Yes, it is true—one of you will betray me." The disciples looked at each other, wondering whom he could mean (vss. 21, 22).

We see here that the sins of those who call themselves Jesus' friends are a cause of great grief to him. The insidious subtlety of sin is something we must guard against. There is tragic solemnity in the account of how Judas is finally excluded from the company of the twelve. What a pitiful picture of unbelief we see in the character of this man. He, like the other disciples, had unsurpassed opportunities to know and learn from Christ; but he cherished his sin of avarice more that the matchless love of Jesus. Significantly, we read that when Judas slunk away it was night (vss. 23–30).

CHRIST'S TABLE TALK

As soon as Judas left the room, Jesus said, "My time has come; the glory of God will soon surround me—and God shall receive great praise because of all that happens to me. And God shall give me his own glory, and this so very soon. Dear, dear children, how brief are these moments before I must go away and leave you! Then, though you search for me, you cannot come to me—just as I told the Jewish leaders.

"And so I am giving a new commandment to you now— love each other just as much as I love you. Your strong love for each other will prove to the world that you are my disciples" (vss. 31–35).

Freed from the presence of the traitor, Judas, we see Jesus opening his heart more fully than he has done before. This is table talk designed to cheer them, to give them the right perspective of the coming suffering and of his death so that they will remember he spoke of it as "glory." He wanted the offense of the cross to cease in their thinking. He knew that in a matter of hours he would be hanging naked, for six hours, between two thieves—and that in all this there would be no appearance of glory. How well he knew that this would be an event calculated to fill their minds with shame, disappointment, and unbelievable heartbreak. But it would result in glory. He drives the point home so that they will not forget it after the first sharp edge of grief and disappointment wear off.

The disciples lean forward, intent on catching every word their dear Master was saying. As Jesus takes into account the serious expression on their faces, noting their perplexity, he calls them *teknia,* "little children." He had never talked to them that way before. It was a word of infinite tenderness, the word his own mother used when she found him (lost) in the Temple (as a child). But it was also a word that recognized peril, and the necessity for care—special care—for the little one.

It is as if he was saying: When I am gone, dear little children, you are going to feel the want of me much like the child who is torn from his mother. You are going to wish you had me with you again, but that cannot be. But this is what you can do to help each other, to make it less difficult for yourselves: Love one another; even as I have loved you.

THE MEANING OF THE NEW COMMANDMENT

Jesus said he was giving a new commandment—not new in the sense that it had not been given before (it was the second great commandment of the law of Moses); but new in the sense that Christ, as the new Lawgiver superseding Moses, in whom the Jews placed such stock, was setting it in its true light. Moses said, "Thou shalt love thy neighbor as thyself" (Lev. 19:18), but Jesus came along and personalized it in a more winning way: "Love each other just as much as I love you." The emphasis is on the *you,* with Christ as the example.

This love is not a common love. Jesus loved even to death. There can be no mistake about these words, this was not merely to be a notion in their heads, but a practice in their lives. The ring of truth resounded in his hearers' ears ever after. Love was to be the grand distinguishing characteristic marking them as Christ's disciples.

Jesus did not talk about gifts, miracles, intellectual attainments, prophecy, tongues, or anything else as being the prerequisite for discipleship. But love, the pure, simple grace of love—a grace within the reach of every believer—this was the one great standard and motive that was to be operative in their experience.

Jesus, the greatest psychologist of all time, knew exactly what this would do when he exalted the value of love to the high pinnacle of calling it "a new commandment." Literally everything hung on the disciples' comprehension of this new dimension of love. Jesus had given his disciples so many instances of his love, but the greatest demonstration lay just ahead. What a test of love it is when a man reaches the point where he is willing to do as Jesus did. Would these disciples pass the test? History has proven that they did. The Christian Church that has come down to us through the centuries is a living testimony to the fact that the disciples excelled in brotherly love. And not only they, but others caught the spirit they demonstrated, so that the early Church flourished and grew. The Word and Christ's love spread through those remarkable eleven men.

Early historians speak of the glory of the primitive church in terms of the love they demonstrated for one another and for others. The constant running theme throughout the New Testament is one of love. No greater emphasis is made on anything than the love that seeks to show the love of Jesus. Adversaries of the early Christians took notice of this love, exclaiming, "See how those Christians love one another!"

There is nothing that grieves my heart more than to see professing Christians acting like cannibals, tearing each other apart, eating each other up with bitter words and unkind deeds. What a disgrace to the cause of Christ!

JESUS FORETELLS PETER'S DENIAL

Simon Peter said, "Master, where are you going?"
And Jesus replied, "You can't go with me now; but you will follow me later."
"But why can't I come now?" he asked, "for I am ready to die for you."
Jesus answered, "Die for me? No—three times before the cock crows tomorrow morning, you will deny that you even know me!" (vs. 36–38).

Peter was bold and blunt in the safety of that Upper Room with Jesus and the other disciples, but in the presence of those who took Christ away he denied knowing Christ. Yet, we know that Peter was destined for martyrdom and that he became one of the great pillars of the early Church.

Matthew Henry remarks that Jesus knows not only the wickedness of sinners, but the weakness of saints. Peter was self-ignorant and over-confident. The marvelous grace of our loving Lord helped Peter to overcome these deficiencies and raised him again after his fall and momentary defection. Jesus never rejected fallible Peter.

20

The Sixth "I Am" and the First Discourse:
Christ the Consoler

The Text: John 14
The Place: The Upper Room in Jerusalem
The Event: Further Instruction from Jesus to His Disciples
             as He Tenderly Commits Them to the Father's
             Care

Although Jesus was standing under the very shadow of the
cross, in self-forgetfulness he comforts his disciples, whose
hearts "were filled with a medley of emotions."

My husband sings a sing that brings tears to the eyes of
many. The title of the song questions: "Who Cares?"

> Who cares when the days are dreary,
> Who cares when I'm tired and weary,
> Jesus my Lord and Saviour cares;
> Who cares when I'm sad and lonely,
> Who cares when I've trouble only,
> Jesus my Lord and Saviour cares.
> There's not a dearer friend to me,
> He'll lead me on till his face I see;
> Who cares when my heart is aching,
> Who cares when it's nearly breaking,
> Jesus my Lord and Saviour cares.
>
> Who cares when my friends forsake me,
> Who cares when the storms o'ertake me,

Jesus my Lord and Saviour cares;
Who cares when my hopes all crumble,
Who cares when I fail and stumble,
Jesus my Lord and Saviour cares.
There's not a dearer friend to me,
He'll lead me on till his face I see;
Who cares when I'm weak and ailing,
Who cares when my strength is failing,
Jesus my Lord and Saviour cares.

John W. Peterson [1]

We need to know that someone cares! There is that inconsolable something within us that cries out for the assurance that we do not stand alone in our time of trouble.

John 14 is regarded by many as the best-loved chapter in the Bible. The first three verses have brought consolation and hope to untold numbers of believers. Sick rooms have been brightened, dying hearts lifted up, and the sorrowing comforted by these matchless words:

"Let not your heart be troubled: ye believe in God, believe also in me.

In my Father's house are many mansions: if it were not so, I would have told you. I go to prepare a place for you.

And if I go and prepare a place for you, I will come again, and receive you unto myself; that where I am, there ye may be also" (John 14:1–3 AV).

That the disciples were troubled was evident to the discerning eye of the Savior. And no wonder! There were a variety of causes contributing to their anxiety. "The hearts of the disciples were filled with a medley of emotions. They were *sad* because of the gloomy prospect of Christ's departure; *ashamed* because of their own demonstrated selfishness and pride; *perplexed* because of the prediction that one of their own number would betray the Master, that another would deny him, and that all would be ensnared because of him; and finally, they

[1] John W. Peterson, *Miracle Melodies* (Grand Rapids, Mich.: Zondervan Publishing House, Singspiration, Inc., 1960), pp. 5, 6.

were *wavering* in their faith, probably thinking: 'How can any one who is about to be betrayed be the Messiah?' Yet, at the same time, they love this Master. They hope against hope. All this is implied in the words, 'Let not your hearts any longer be troubled.' " [2]

At the close of the previous chapter Jesus told Peter he was going to deny him three times. What fearful discouragement must have rolled over the soul of Peter! Jesus looked ahead and saw the horrible guilt that Peter would feel; days and nights of restless tossing when Peter found himself practically gagging in grief and bitter remorse. Jesus looked at disconsolate Peter, he looked at the other disciples, knowing the shame they would feel after they had fled from his enemies, and he saw far into the future, knowing the persecution and suffering they would endure at the hands of wicked men. So many times the future would loom as dark and foreboding: they would be hunted like wild animals, know hunger, cold, sickness, and aching loneliness. Between grace and glory they would drink many bitter cups. But he had the remedy against this trouble of mind. The prescription has stood the test of time.

Who among us can't identify with Peter? The stress of circumstances does knock us about, and we lose our balance. We are like a drowning man flailing about. We go down feeling that we will never come back up. We know that we have denied our Lord in acts if not in words. Or we have left unsaid and undone those things that we know were expected of us.

Jesus' disciples were so earthbound in their thinking; we are not unlike them. These men were not unique in their disposition to being melancholy on occasion, or introspective. Failure and mistakes marred their walk. They suffered from the age-old disease of heart-trouble. Some of it was by their own doing; other causes contributed, leaving them pained and sorrowful. Does it not all sound familiar? The fogs and difficulties of our increasingly hostile environment cloud our perspective and obscure our vision. If the disciples needed

[2] William Henriksen, *The Gospel of John* (Grand Rapids, Mich.: Baker Bk. House, 1953), p. 263.

Jesus' message to comfort their troubled hearts, surely we need it.

There Are Accommodations in Heaven for the Saints

Although the disciples had faith, it was beginning to waver. There are degrees in faith; weak faith may save a man, but it will not give much comfort in time of trouble. Jesus sought to reinforce the disciples' faith in him. He recognized that they had faith and trust in God, so he urges upon them the necessity to keep on trusting in him as well.

Heaven is a prepared place for a prepared people. Here Jesus says that he is going on ahead to make Heaven ready for our arrival. You can rest assured that when you enter Heaven, you are neither unknown nor unexpected. There are accommodations in Heaven for the saints of the Lord.

> "And you know where I am going and how to get there."
> "No, we don't," Thomas said. "We haven't any idea where you are going, so how can we know the way?" (vss. 4, 5).

The Way to the Father

Dear Thomas, magnificently honest. He would in no way pretend. Bluntly, he contradicted Jesus, affording Jesus the opportunity to utter that great claim:

> "I am the way, the truth, and the life: no man cometh unto the Father, but by me" (vs. 6 AV).

In this great I AM Jesus is saying that he will not merely show us the way, but that he is the way. Not only does he have love, but he is love. God is always equal to each of his attributes

The Deep Underlying Want of Humanity

Then we hear another voice, that of Philip. It is as if he is rushing to the defense of Thomas.

"Sir, show us the Father and we will be satisfied" (vs. 8).

I never read that without amazement. Jesus had been their closest companion for three years, intimately conversant with them, and yet Philip, acting as spokesman for the others, comes up with this request. Jesus' disappointment shows in his reproof as he, too, expresses amazement (vss. 9–11).

Philip was actually asking for a theophany—a visible manifestation of the Father's glory such as had been granted to Moses and other believers in the old dispensation (Ex. 24:9–11; 33:18). How he erred! A far greater privilege than that which Moses experienced had been given to him and the other disciples.

JESUS MAKES THREE PROMISES TO SILENCE THEIR FEARS

Not only were the disciples full of grief at the thought of Jesus' parting, but they were full of care as they wondered what would become of themselves after his departure. Knowing full well the thoughts and intents of their hearts and minds, Jesus goes on to give them instructions regarding their future course and makes three promises peculiarly suited to their circumstances each designed to cheer them.

The three promises are in regard to works, prayer, and power. There would be power on earth (vs. 12), power in heaven (vs. 13), and power indwelling them through the Holy Spirit (vss. 15–17).

THE FIRST PROMISE: REGARDING WORKS

The first promise assured them that just because he was leaving them, this would not mean an end to miraculous works and they would not be left weak and helpless and unable to do anything to arrest the attention of the unbelieving world. Just as the Father confirmed the Son's words by works (signs, miracles), he would take care that believers would have that same power. He even went so far as to tell them they would do "greater" works. Certainly this must have perked up their ears!

Hadn't Jesus healed the sick, cleansed the leper, given sight to the blind, raised the dead? Did Jesus actually mean they would be able to do those things *and more*! Christ healed with the hem of his garment, Peter with his shadow (Acts 5:15); Paul effected healing by the use of a handkerchief (Acts 19:12). Jesus performed many miracles for the brief years of his public ministry, but his followers wrought miracles in his name all over the world (and such divine power is still at work today).

What were the *greater works* to which Jesus referred? This is in reference to the converting of souls. There is no miracle quite so great as the transformation that comes into an individual's life when he comes from the darkness of sin into the Light of the knowledge of Jesus. This believers in every age can rightfully claim as their promise of power.

THE SECOND PROMISE: PRAYER

The second promise had to do with prayer. Jesus elevates prayer to the proper place it must hold in the life of a believer. How could they keep up communion with him? Through prayer. Prayer is our avenue of communication with the Father through the Son. "Let me hear from you by prayer," is what Jesus was saying. "You are my friends, I am your friend, let's keep in close touch." How little we use the means of power at our disposal! What spiritual paupers we are through neglect and ignorance!

There was only one qualification: they were to ask in Jesus' name. Why do some have prayers answered, while others seemingly never experience this power working on their behalf? It has to do with their relationship to the Son. Do they belong in the Father's family? Access to the Father-heart of God comes through believing in and accepting his Son; this then assures an individual of audience with a prayer-hearing and a prayer-answering God.

THE THIRD PROMISE: THE COMFORTER

The third promise is a striking one. This is the first time
the Holy Ghost is mentioned as Christ's special gift to his
own. Our safety, peace, and power as believers is all tied up
in recognition and acceptance of Jesus' teachings regarding
the one he calls "the Comforter."

At the 1974 Congress on World Evangelization held in
Lausanne, Switzerland, Billy Graham in the opening message
to the delegates said: "It is foolish and vain to try to do
God's work without God's power. But there is no way for
Christians to have God's power except by prayer. Evangelism
is always in danger of succumbing to a humanistic activity.
Successful evangelism, whatever method may be used, must
be saturated in prayer. For ten days prior to Pentecost the
disciples 'continued with one accord in prayer and supplica-
tion.' Their prayers were heard. The Spirit descended. The
power abounded. Weak men became strong. Faithless men
became faithful. Speechless men spoke the Word with power
and, most glorious of all, sinners who listened became saints
through faith in the risen Christ.

"If prayer is a basic need for evangelism, a second need is
that we be filled with the power of the Holy Spirit. Only a
Spirit-filled people can finish the job of world evangelization.
It is the Holy Spirit who convicts of sin, righteousness and
judgment, and who performs the work of regeneration. It is
the Holy Spirit who indwells believers, who guides, teaches,
instructs. He is the great Communicator of the Gospel. He
uses ordinary people as his instruments, but it is his work.
When the Gospel is faithfully declared, it is the Holy Spirit
who sends it like a fiery dart into the hearts of those who
have been prepared.

"Storm clouds are gathering. Satan is marshaling his forces
for his fiercest attack in history. Ours is a cosmic struggle.
Satan will do everything he can to discourage, divide and
defeat us, as we seek to carry out the Great Commission of
our Lord. But we follow the Son of God who has already

nullified the powers of death, hell and Satan; and the final victory is certain." [3]

The gift of the Holy Spirit distinguishes in a peculiar way those who belong to Christ. The great distinction between the children of God and the children of the world can be seen right here. What a Comforter he is! What a power!

One of the saddest things to see is an orphaned child. Here Jesus uses that term, promising his disciples and all who believe that they will not be like orphans.

THE LEGACY JESUS BEQUEATHED

But there was still more—what a rich giver Jesus was and is!

> "I am leaving you with a gift—peace of mind and heart! And the peace I give isn't fragile like the peace the world gives. So don't be troubled or afraid" (vs. 27).

Could anyone ask for a greater legacy than that? *Peace!* Individuals and nations desperately crave peace. And it is theirs merely for the asking and receiving. He, Jesus, is our way of peace (Eph. 2:14). He is the composure of our minds.

Matthew Henry in describing this legacy of love says: "When Christ was about to leave the world he made his will. His soul he committed to his Father; his body he bequeathed to Joseph, to be decently interred; his clothes fell to the soldiers; his mother he left to the care of John: but what should he leave to his poor disciples, that had left all for him? Silver and gold he had none; but he left them that which was infinitely better, *his peace*. '*I leave you, but* I leave *my peace* with you. I not only give you a title to it, but put you in possession of it.' He did not part in anger, but in love; for this was his farewell, *Peace I leave with you,* as a dying father

---

[3] Billy Graham, "Let the Earth Hear His Voice," *Decision* Magazine, October 1974, p. 12.

leaves portions to his children; and this is a *worthy portion*."
(italics Matthew Henry's.)[4]

Jesus never promised his disciples and future followers
that the way to heaven would be paved with riches. But he
did promise something far more valuable: *his peace.* This
inheritance is for all believers. Let us claim it.

But even while Jesus was speaking these blessed words
that have brought so much help and hope to believers, he
was aware of the distant *tramp, tramp* of the approaching
enemy. The Roman soldiers, Temple police, members of the
Sanhedrin, and yes, Judas, all of them under the domination
of Satan, were on their way to capture Jesus. They came as
if they were going to take captive an exceedingly dangerous
criminal, with swords, sticks, lanterns, torches, and other
weapons. Knowing this, Jesus sets his disciples' minds at rest
and tells them "they have no power over me, but I freely will
hand myself over to them."

[4] *Matthew Henry's Commentary, Vol. V.,* p. 1119.

21

The Seventh "I Am" and the Second Discourse: Christ the Vine

The Text: John 15
The Place: Jerusalem the Night Before Christ's Crucifixion
The Event: Further Words from Jesus in Admonition and
            Prediction

There is no higher goal to which you can aspire than to reflect the self-sacrificing nature of Jesus' love. A friend of Jesus will exhibit his peace, his joy, and his love. These are some of the "fruits" that come as a result of abiding in him, the true Vine.

Life without the physical presence of Jesus would be an abrupt change for the disciples. They had become accustomed and conditioned to the strength of his presence. Now, suddenly, they were to be plunged into the abyss of loneliness and despair.

Jesus would further prepare their hearts with teaching that would lodge in their minds and hearts to be recalled later when they needed it most, and that would help to fortify them for all that lay ahead. He chose his words with care. The kind of loving caring that characterized his concern, using the analogy of the vine.

"I am the true vine, and my Father is the vinedresser.
"Every branch in me that does not bear fruit, he takes

away; and every *branch* that bears fruit, he prunes it, that it may bear more fruit.

"You are already clean because of the word which I have spoken to you.

"Abide in me, and I in you. As the branch cannot bear fruit of itself, unless it abides in the vine, so neither can you, unless you abide in me.

"I am the vine, you are the branches; he who abides in me, and I in him, he bears much fruit; for apart from me you can do nothing.

"If anyone does not abide in me, he is thrown away as a branch, and dries up; and they gather them, and cast them into the fire and they are burned.

"If you abide in me, and my words abide in you, ask whatever you wish, and it shall be done for you.

"By this is my Father glorified, that you bear much fruit, and so prove to be my disciples" (John 15:1–8 NAS).

The figure of speech with reference to the vine was not a new one. Old Testament teaching and literature of the disciples' day was saturated with teaching and illustrative symbolism all employing the figure of the vine.

It was God's glorious intent that the nation of Israel bear fruit for him before all the nations of the world. Hosea the prophet sadly said, "Israel is an empty vine" (Hos. 10). There was no real fruit for God. Isaiah pictured the vine as bringing forth wild grapes. That was failure. Jeremiah came along and dismally spoke of the nation as being a "a degenerate vine." And so God rejected that earthly vine. They bore fruit only unto themselves, rejecting the Messiah in their midst, refusing to testify to the truth that he was the Savior sent into the world.

The relationship between Jesus and those who would be his disciples is like that of a vine and its branches. He is the true source of all life and spiritual vigor. Disciples of Jesus in any age are entirely dependent on him, just as branches on the vine are to the parent stem. Jesus called God "the vinedresser" (i.e., the husbandman), explaining that the Father takes the same tender interest in his disciples as the vinedresser does in the branch of the vine. The fertility and fruitfulness of the vine and its branches are the concern of the husbandman. Just so, the Father is deeply interested in our spiritual welfare and usefulness. The vine and branches exist for fruitage. The vine needs the branch for fruitage; but the branch needs the vine for the production of fruit. The relationship is one of perfect unity.

But there is a process involved that results in fruitage: pruning, cutting out fruitless branches and burning them, and then the purging and cleansing of remaining branches so that they may be more fruitful. Anyone who has worked with vines knows the process. If a gardener cannot get results from certain branches, he is justified in cutting away unproductive growth. And in order to ensure maximum yield, the vinedresser deals with the fruit-bearing branches, removing any hindering thing so that more fruit may be attained.

ABIDING, ESSENTIAL TO LIFE

The condition for spiritual usefulness and maximum "fruit-bearing" is identical with the natural one—abiding in the vine. When a good branch is severed from the vine, it will produce nothing, even though it was good. Union with Christ, the true Vine, is incomparably necessary to that one who hopes to bring forth fruit. "Apart from me," Jesus said, "you can do nothing."

You can count on it, God will generate all that is necessary for your spiritual growth and full productivity if you are abiding in Christ, the true Vine, the root and source of all your help and hope.

"My true disciples produce bountiful harvests. This brings great glory to my Father.

"I have loved you even as the Father has loved me. Live within my love. When you obey me you are living in my love, just as I obey my Father and live in his love. I have

told you this so that you will be filled with my joy. Yes,
your cup of joy will overflow!" (vss. 4–11).

A New Intimacy in the Love-mastered Life

It comes almost as a shock to hear Jesus speaking of "my
joy." This is the eve of his crucifixion. Without a doubt this
arrested the thoughts of his disciples. Here they were with
their beloved friend approaching the hour he had often
alluded to, which they now somehow, though not completely,
understood would be an hour of death and suffering, and he
speaks of the cup of joy.

What is that joy? Jesus' joy was in doing the will of the
Father in answer to the love of the Father. To enter into that
experience we must abide in his love and be a channel of
that love to others. The more we overflow, the greater the
joy and the more there will be an inflow.

> "I demand that you love each other as much as I love you.
> And here is how to measure it—the greatest love is shown
> when a person lays down his life for his friends, and you are
> my friends if you obey me. I no longer call you slaves, for
> a master doesn't confide in his slaves; now you are my
> friends, proved by the fact that I have told you everything
> the Father told me" (vss. 12–15).

How did their hearts respond to this new revelation of
intimacy? I believe they began to search their innermost
feelings as the spotlight of Jesus' love shone on them. To be
called the friend of Jesus is no small matter. What a privilege!
Intentionally, he calls their attention to the fact that he is
their friend. Soon they were to know the enmity of the world;
many of their former friends would desert them. They would
never need to say, "I have no friend left to turn to."

Do you take comfort in the fact of Jesus' friendship? Our
earthly friends may fail, but Jesus is the dearest and most
faithful Friend who will never forsake us.

JESUS WARNS OF THE WORLD'S HATRED

The world is at enmity with those who are followers of Christ. Christian love is placed in contrast to the hatred of the world (vss. 16–27), and the picture is one of persecution, ridicule, mockery, slander, misrepresentation—all that is in opposition to God and his revealed truth.

Persecution has been the lot of the followers of Christ in every age. It is believed that not more than one or two of the first disciples and their companions probably died quietly in bed. Persecution. Suffering. Martyrdom. Union with Christ the Vine means fellowship with him in suffering in this world. It costs something to be a Christian. It cost the Son his life and his disciples unbelievable persecution and suffering. What is it costing you?

22

The Third Discourse:
The Spirit's Work

The Text: John 16
The Place: Somewhere in Jerusalem the Night Before Christ's Crucifixion
The Event: Jesus Alone with His Disciples, Giving Private Teaching to Fortify Them for the Work Ahead

The early Church lived dangerously. There was what J. B. Phillips calls "a suprahuman power" working through and energizing them and exerting a widespread influence. There was an excitement that was contagious; an unconquerable fellowship; an active, energetic Spirit of truth present, with the courage to match their new vision. Whatever "it" was, "it" worked, moving in on the human scene with astonishing impact.

G. K. Chesterton has made the observation that whatever else man is, he is not what he was meant to be. The question is in order: Why?

J. B. Phillips offers this explanation: "I am convinced that there will be no recovery of the vitality and vigor of New Testament Christianity until we who call ourselves Christians dare to break through contemporary habits of thought and touch the resources of God." [1]

[1] J. B. Phillips, *New Testament Christianity* (New York: The Macmillan Co., 1957), p. 32.

In the previous chapter, after Jesus had warned his disciples of the enmity they could expect from the world, he added an important "but."

"But I will send you the Comforter—the Holy Spirit, the source of all truth" (John 15:26a).

Here is the resource J. B. Phillips and others are referring to. The God-given vigor of the early Church came in direct proportion to their recognition of this and a new love-energy was released in quantity and quality.

THE WORLD'S DARKNESS

Jesus wanted his disciples and succeeding generations of believers to know and understand just what they would be expected to go through in this world because they belonged to him.

"I have told you these things so that you won't be staggered (by all that lies ahead). For you will be excommunicated from the synagogues, and indeed the time is coming when those who kill you will think they are doing God a service. This is because they have never known the Father or me. Yes, I am telling you these things now so that when they happen you will remember I warned you. I didn't tell you earlier because I was going to be with you for a while longer. But I am now going away to the one who sent me; and none of you seems interested in the purpose of my going; none wonders why. Instead you are only filled with sorrow. But the fact of the matter is that it is best for you that I go away, for if I don't, the Comforter won't come. If I do, he will—for I will send him to you" (John 16:1–7).

The violence of opposition the followers of Christ endured came just as Jesus had revealed it would. The early Church was compelled to form close-knit fellowships in order to survive against forces of paganism and those with false zeal wielding the sword of ecclesiastical censure.

Jesus dealt faithfully with his disciples, for he wanted them to know and count the cost. By giving them notice of what was ahead, he removed some of the terror so that they would not be taken wholly by surprise.

Jesus showed the reason for the world's hostility:

"The world's sin is unbelief in me" (vs. 9).

THE PROMISE OF GUIDANCE AND HELP

"There is righteousness available because I go to the Father and you shall see me no more; there is deliverance from judgment because the prince of this world has already been judged" (vss. 10, 11).

This is real warfare. Some of us are actively engaged in combat. Not a day goes by but what my husband and I don't question each other: "How goes the battle?" We know who our enemy is and why he will not leave us alone. There are advances and then discouraging setbacks. Victories. Temporary defeats. But we know that God's Son will always triumph over these forces. Jesus said, "There is deliverance." We have seen it, experienced it, and can testify that what our Savior said is true.

Francis A. Schaeffer emphasizes that the greatest battles in the Christian life in the realm of true spirituality rest in the realm of our thought-life. If Satan succeeds in darkening my thoughts, he is gaining ground. "The work of the Holy Spirit, as the agent of the Trinity, is not a coat we put on. It is not an external thing at all, but internal, bringing in turn something external. . . .

"In our thought-world, we are to bow under the work of the Holy Spirit internally, and then as we, in active passivity, give up ourselves to him, the fruit of the resurrected and glorified Christ flows forth through our bodies into the external world." [2]

---

[2] Francis A. Schaeffer, *True Spirituality* (Wheaton, Ill.: Tyndale House Publishers, 1971), p. 119.

Christ has said and done enough to fill all our hearts with joy forevermore, but by looking only at the magnitude of our problems and that which is against us, we so crowd our hearts and our thinking, that there is left no room for joy—his joy (John 15:11). We hinder the effective operation of the work of the Holy Spirit on our behalf when we dwell on what Christ called "our sorrows." In gaining the disciples' attention, Jesus employs use of the word "expedient," which carried arresting meaning.

"It is expedient for you that I go away" (John 16:7a AV).

It is to your advantage is what he was saying. Jesus could not be everywhere present at once in his bodily form. It was thus necessary that he voluntarily leave this world. "My going is a gain. The physical intimacy we have enjoyed is as nothing in comparison to that which will begin when the Comforter comes."

THREEFOLD WORK OF THE SPIRIT EXPLAINED

The witness of the Holy Spirit in the world has to do with three things: sin, righteousness, judgment (vss. 8, 12–16). Men under the influence of the Spirit will recognize their sins, all that is out of step and not in harmony with the revealed Truth. They will gain a right understanding of righteousness, that is, the human life of Jesus and that which corresponds to the nature and will of God. And the Holy Spirit will convince the world that all judgment is committed to him, that Satan, subdued by Christ, has had the sentence of judgment already passed upon him, and that on the final day of judgment all the obstinate enemies of Christ will be reckoned with.

THE PROMISE OF JOY

The disciples were frail and faulty, they failed to apprehend all his teaching. Jesus showed once again how much he cared—he gives just as much as he knows we are capable of bearing.

"Whatever is he saying?" some of his disciples asked. "What is this about 'going to the Father'? We don't know what he means."
Jesus realized they wanted to ask him so he said, "Are you asking yourselves what I mean? The world will greatly rejoice over what is going to happen to me, and you will weep. But your weeping shall suddenly be turned to wonderful joy (when you see me again). It will be the same joy as that of a woman in labor when her child is born— her anguish gives place to rapturous joy and the pain is forgotten. You have sorrow now, but I will see you again and then you will rejoice; and no one can rob you of that joy. At that time you won't need to ask me for anything, for you can go directly to the Father and ask him, and he will give you what you ask for because you use my name. You haven't tried this before (but begin now). Ask, using my name, and you will receive, and your cup of joy will overflow" (vss. 19–24).

He gives them an easy-to-understand illustration, that of a woman giving birth to a baby. In another book I state: "The pain of giving birth is quickly replaced with the joy of receiving a child from the Lord—our very own baby!"[3] You talk about joy! What exquisite joy that is! "The effort and pain are quickly forgotten in the great joy that overwhelms you as you hear that longed-for first cry of your new-born child."[4] It is not difficult for us as women to understand Jesus' reference here to joy—rapturous joy.

ENCOURAGING FAREWELL WORDS

"I have spoken of these matters very guardedly, but the time will come when this will not be necessary and I will tell you plainly all about the Father. Then you will present your petitions over my signature! And I won't need to ask the Father to grant you these requests, for the Father himself loves you dearly because you love me and believe that I came from the Father. Yes, I came from the Father into the world and will leave the world and return to the Father" (vss. 25–30).

Nativity and Incarnation; mission, teaching, and ministry; ascension and return to glory—it's all there. This is the end and scope of his parting address. He has pointed backward to his identification with humanity; and he points forward to his resurrection into glory. And suddenly, it is as if a giant spotlight has beamed into their midst, and we hear them exclaiming:

"At last you are speaking plainly," his disciples said, "and not in riddles. Now we understand that you know everything and don't need anyone to tell you anything. From this we believe that you came from God" (vss. 29, 30).

THE FINAL WORD OF STRENGTH

"Do you finally believe this?" Jesus asked. "But the time is coming—in fact, it is here—when you will be scattered, each one returning to his own home, leaving me alone. Yet I will not be alone, for the Father is with me. I have told you all this so that you will have peace of heart and mind. Here on earth you will have many trials and sorrows; but cheer up, for I have overcome the world" (vss. 31–33).

He had spoken some wounding words to his disciples; but also healing words. Both were needful. Both were said out of the depths of his loving heart.

I am most impressed with what J. B. Phillips says in regard to the peace that distinguished the young Church of which these disciples were leaders: "As we study New Testament Christianity we are aware that there is an inner core of tranquillity and stability. In fact, not the least of the impressive qualities which the Church could demonstrate to the pagan world was this ballast of inward peace. It was, I think, something new that was appearing in the lives of human beings. It was not mere absence of strife or conflict, and certainly not the absence of what ordinarily makes for anxiety; nor was it a lack of sensitivity or a complacent self-satisfaction, which can often produce an apparent tranquillity of spirit. It was a positive peace, a solid foundation which held fast amid all the turmoil of human experience. It was, in short, the experience of Christ's bequest when He said, 'Peace I leave with you, my peace I give unto you: not as the world giveth, give I unto you.' (John 14:27)" [5]

Once again, in these his final words he underscores this legacy that is his bequest: Perfect peace and confidence. It's yours and it's mine. *Thank you, Jesus, for caring!*

[5] *New Testament Christianity*, p. 79.

23

The Prayer of the Word:
The Great Intercessor

The Text: John 17
The Place: Somewhere in or near Jerusalem Shortly Before Jesus' Betrayal and Arrest
The Event: God (the Son) Conversing with God (the Father), Often Called Christ's High-Priestly Intercessory Prayer

There are some matters that must be settled in the loneliness of a man's own soul as he lifts up his eyes to heaven seeking to know the will of the Father. It is this kind of praying that confronts us in John 17, where we hear Jesus praying as a man to his heavenly Father. In this portrait of Jesus in prayer we are privileged to listen in on a conversation that took place inside the Trinity. This is God (the Son) conversing with God (the Father).

Morgan comments: "I would ever be careful lest I should appear to differentiate between the value of one part of Holy Scripture and another, but no one will deny that when we come to this chapter we are at the centre of all the sanctities." [1]

"Jesus' High-Priestly prayer has been called the New Testament's noblest and purest pearl of devotion." [2]

[1] G. Campbell Morgan, *The Gospel According to John*, p. 266.
[2] Irving L. Jensen, *John, A Self-Study Guide* (Chicago: Moody Press, 1970), p. 87.

The prayer itself can be divided into three main parts: Jesus prays for himself (John 17: 1–8); for his disciples (vss. 9–19); and for the Church (vss. 20–26).

THE SON REPORTING TO THE FATHER: MISSION ACCOMPLISHED

This is the prayer of complete and unblemished faith, the report of finished work (vss. 1–8). It is a prayer of glory, too, not self-glory, but for the Father's glory. Even Christ, as man, must correspond and communicate with Heaven through prayer. If he, how much more we!

Jesus uses the word *Father* six times in this one prayer. There is no request for strength for the extremely difficult hours ahead, and there is not even a request for guidance; it is simply the son reporting to the Father in the intimacy of the family circle.

As Jesus speaks of glory once again, it comes as a shock to realize that the reference is to the cross. What could be more ugly and degrading than death on the cross? Humanly speaking, who would want to die on a cross suspended in midair for all the world to gaze upon? The agony—both physical and mental (in contemplation)—cannot be comprehended. And who would wish to die at thirty-three? But the glory to which Jesus referred encompassed not only his impending death, but the glorious sequel shown in his resurrection power and ascension majesty.

To see Jesus, on his knees, earnestly asking the Father for the cross and his and his Father's glory, is to see the Son longing to be restored to the Father's presence—the Son away from Home (Heaven).

JESUS PRAYING FOR THOSE WHO ARE HIS

"My plea is not for the world but for those you have given me because they belong to you. And all of them, since they are mine, belong to you; and you have given them back to me with everything else of yours, and so *they are my glory!*

Now I am leaving the world, and leaving them behind, and coming to you. Holy Father, keep them in your own care—all those you have given me—so that they will be united just as we are, with none missing. During my time here I have kept safe within your family all of these you gave me. I guarded them so that not one perished, except the son of hell, as the Scriptures foretold.

"And now I am coming to you. I have told them these things while I was with them so that they would be filled with my joy. I have given them your commands. And the world hates them because they don't fit in with it, just as I don't. I'm not asking you to take them out of the world, but to keep them safe from Satan's power. They are not part of this world any more than I am. Make them pure and holy through teaching them your words of truth. As you sent me into the world, I am sending them into the world, and I consecrate myself to meet their need for growth in truth and holiness" (vss. 9–19).

Jesus does things for those who are his that he does not do for unbelievers. What comfort there is in that fact! "I pray for them," he says, and there it is in black and white, "I pray not for the world." The world doesn't like to hear that, but it is true. The Son cannot be complacent about sin, he cannot wink at the evil deeds and thoughts of unbelievers. Christ loves the sinner; that teaching is clear in the Word, and he demonstrated it in his earthly life, but he intercedes only for those who come unto God by him.

There is safety and grand assurance in that for the believer. We are daily watched, thought about, and provided for with unfailing care by that one who, the Bible tells us, never slumbers nor sleeps. This is one of the peculiar privileges of believers.

It was fitting that Christ should pray specifically for his disciples, who were to be the instrumentality by which the world would be won for Christ. Therefore, Christ asks three things for these men: "Holy Father, keep them in your own care" (vs. 11); "Keep them safe from Satan's power" (vs.

15b); and "Make them pure and holy through teaching them your words of truth" (vs. 17).

Each petition relates to spiritual blessings in regard to heavenly things. Jesus does not pray that they might be rich and great in the world (Matthew Henry says that prosperity of the soul is the best prosperity), but his request is that they might be furnished and equipped with that which will move them along the path of duty to him, and which will result in their being brought safely to heaven.

Jesus requests that the Father keep these disciples that "they may be one, as we are." He did not want them broken up, weakened, and paralyzed by internal strife and divisions.

Jesus' next plea makes mention again of the hostile world. We are in a perilous position as believers, because the world hates Christ and therefore it hates us. But let us take special note of what Jesus says: "I do not ask thee to take them out of the world, but to keep them from the evil one" (vs. 15). What an encouragement that is! We can be in this world and not a part of it because we are sustained by the power of the prayer of the Son of God.

When you are knocked down (inwardly speaking) by the world and by Christians who are not living as one in unity with the Father and the Son, and when unkind, untrue things are said about you, how do you keep on keeping on? You remember what Jesus prayed to the Father.

Does he hear? Does Jesus care? Ah yes, from the depths of human experience you can take my word for it; but not mine only—look into the pages of the blessed Word of God; see there the suffering these saints endured at the hands of the world (those outside of Christ) and those who, in the name of religion, persecuted them. Did God keep them? What would have happened to the cause of Christ if God had not answered the Son's prayer? Look around—see what Christianity has done for the world; see how it has spread from one end of the globe to the other.

It is for the benefit of the world that we must expect trouble, conflict, and even persecution. How else is the world to know the power of Christ if we do not demonstrate God's keeping power? Therefore, we are to count it a joy, a privilege, a responsibility not to be taken lightly, when we are confronted with attacks from the evil one. We are to stand firm in the power of Christ, and thus to bring glory to God. God can be counted upon to see us through these battles.

Corrie ten Boom says: "People are going through difficult times now. But in the life of a child of God, when the worst happens, the best remains." That from the lips of one of God's choicest saints who knows from bitter firsthand experience whereof she speaks.[3]

Then, finally, Jesus prays, "Sanctify them through thy truth: thy word is truth" (vs. 17 AV). More and more, I am coming to see, as I persevere in this walk of faith, that the only way I am going to be kept is as I draw upon the resources provided *in* the Word and *by* the Word (Jesus). I deprive myself of spiritual benefits when I do not feed upon this blessed Word. I am wasted and weak apart from the Word. Jesus said it and I claim it: *"I consecrate myself to meet their need for growth in truth and holiness"* (vs. 19. [italics author's]).

JESUS PRAYING FOR YOU AND ME

"I am not praying for these alone but also for the future believers who will come to me because of the testimony of these. My prayer for all of them is that they will be of one heart and mind, just as you and I are, Father—that just as you are in me and I am in you, so they will be in us, and the world will believe you sent me.

"I have given them the glory you gave me—the glorious unity of being one, as we are—I in them and you in me, all being perfected into one—so that the world will know you sent me and will understand that you love them as much as you love me. Father, I want them with me—these you've given me—so that they can see my glory. You

---

[3] Miss ten Boom is that saint the Lord is using mightily all over the world through her speaking, her books, and now the film of her life, adapted from her autobiography *The Hiding Place*. (The film is produced by Worldwide Pictures.) She is the Dutch evangelist who was incarcerated in Ravensbruck concentration camp during part of World War II.

gave me the glory because you loved me before the world began! Oh righteous Father, the world doesn't know you, but I do; and these disciples know you sent me. And I have revealed you to them, and will keep on revealing you so that the mighty love you have for me may be in them, and I in them" (vss. 20–26).

Jesus, in his last movement in this prayer petition to the Father, looked beyond the men immediately surrounding him, through the vista of the coming centuries, and saw in one comprehensive glance all that the Father was going to give him— those who would be gathered to him through the message and the ministry of these for whom he had been praying. Jesus saw and prayed for us!

PART IV

Obedience, Even Unto Death

24

Countdown for Crucifixion:
Courageous and Compcsed

The Text: John 18:1–27
The Place: The Garden of Gethsemane and the Court of
the High Priest
The Event: The Betrayal and Arrest; the Preliminary Hearing and "Ecclesiastical" Trial

Do you want to know the grand secret of living at peace with
yourself and others? It is this: Form the habit of laying everything before the Lord in prayer and asking him to choose the
way for you. Then, can you learn to step out of the way so
he can have his way? It is not a matter of retreating into a do-
nothing manner of living; it is not throwing up your hands
and saying God will answer prayer and God will provide.
There is a fine line between *submission* of one's will to the
will of God and *doing* the will of the Lord. Release and waiting call for patience. But it also requires using that which
God has already provided: one's intelligence and doing what
is necessary and near at hand, using the resources one pos-
sesses, the knowledge and understanding that God gives. It
involves stepping out in this matter of believing faith.

Jesus, in the preceding chapter, showed that preparation
through prayer preceded his great work in submission to the
will of the Father. Remember that as you are confronted with
the "dailyness" of living and the difficult decisions you must

153

make, as well as the sufferings you will be called upon at times to endure. Learn from Jesus in these his final movements in his great mission of manifestation. Watch carefully as he enters the Divinely programmed final countdown on his way to the cross.

JESUS IN THE GARDEN

Strengthened by prayer, Jesus and his followers went forth into a garden (John 18:1). Prayer such as Jesus prayed will always give way to action. It is possible to advance on one's knees. Jesus arose from praying to meet his great ordeal.

The three Synoptic writers tell of the agony Christ suffered, with sweat falling to the ground like great drops of blood. Christ's body was racked with pain as he faced thoughts of what lay ahead. When you are almost overwhelmed by the vicissitudes of life, don't forget that Jesus has been there! This garden spot that Jesus chose was a familiar refuge.

Judas, the betrayer, knew this place, for Jesus had gone there many times with his disciples (vs. 2).

Judas stands as a glaring example of the temporary triumph of selfishness and sin. Judas betrayed Jesus with a kiss—that caress with the lips that we give to those whom we love—selling him for a few pieces of silver. Avarice. Greed. *Sin.* Judas was a man who cherished a besetting sin and yielded to it in evil passion.

The chief priests and Pharisees had given Judas a squad of soldiers and police to accompany him. Now with blazing torches, lanterns, and weapons they arrived at the olive grove (vs. 3).

I find that amazing. The enemies of Christ came seeking the Light of the world with blazing torches and lanterns! Their own thinking and the darkness of their evil deed caused them to suspect that Christ and his followers would run for hiding or offer resistance.

What are we to learn from this? Jesus is Master of every situation. Even though dreadful things are thrust upon us—our own personal agony and crosses—Jesus did not try to escape or evade his agony and the cross but grasped it firmly and went through it nobly, bravely, manfully. Can we do the same in his power? The cross became glory for Christ. God vindicated him. Circumstances may come into our lives, often at the hands of others who mean it for evil, but God intends it for good. God will allow us to be brought into difficulties, not that he necessarily intends this, but because evil men plot it, and sin causes it, but if we place ourselves in his hands, he will magnify himself and be our Deliverer.

The number of men who came to arrest Jesus is also surprising. These were Roman soldiers lent by Pilate to the priests for the occasion, and Temple police—two bitterly opposed parties theologically and politically, united in their determination to put an end to Jesus.

But all of this show of power was an enormous waste of energy. In striking contrast to the hideous spectacle of Judas, we see Jesus voluntarily offering himself to his enemies. He was not a Victim; he was a Victor. They couldn't have hurt a hair on his head if he hadn't allowed it. Think back and recall how when the people wanted to take him by force to make him a king, he withdrew and hid himself (John 6:15); now, however, when they come to take him by force to put him to death, he offers himself.

> Jesus fully realized all that was going to happen to him. Stepping forward to meet them he asked, "Whom are you looking for?"
> "Jesus of Nazareth," they replied.
> "I am he," Jesus said. And as he said it, they all fell backwards to the ground! (vss. 4–6).

He could have struck them down dead. Such was his power! But no! He strides forth with majesty and faces them, not waiting for them to challenge him or command him to surrender. Down that "great multitude of men" went, slain under the power of Jesus. When they struggled to their feet, still stunned,

> Once more he asked them, "Whom are you searching for?"
> And again they replied, "Jesus of Nazareth."
> "I told you I am he," Jesus said; "and since I am the one you are after, let these others go." He did this to carry out the prophecy he had just made, "I have not lost a single one of those you gave me . . ." (vss. 7–9).

You cannot help but be impressed with the dignity and calmness of Jesus as he patiently and courageously deals with his enemies. But his concern is for his disciples. Both he and his disciples could have fled while the soldiers and police lay flat on their backs.

Jesus knows our hearts; he knows exactly how much we can stand under pressure. He will not give us more than we can bear. He knew that if the disciples were taken prisoners at this point, they would break down. There would have been shipwreck of their faith. We can rest on that for ourselves: God *will* take care of us. Jesus' word to his enemies had a ring of authority that they did not dispute, and the lives of his disciples were spared, but at the last moment Simon Peter does something rash.

> Then Simon Peter drew a sword and slashed off the right ear of Malchus, the High Priest's servant.
> But Jesus said to Peter, "Put your sword away. Shall I not drink from the cup the Father has given me?" (vss. 10, 11).

Dear impetuous Peter! He acted impulsively and hastily, but with blundering zeal. He was always demonstrative and fervent, but this time when he let go, he missed. Undoubtedly he was aiming for the man's head. Peter was not a swordsman, but a fisherman! Jesus saw into Peter's heart; he recognized the motive that prompted this big foolish fisherman to lash out. There is a warning here: Zeal without knowledge can be dangerous to the cause of Christ. Peter almost frustrated the purpose of Jesus and compromised his cause—

except for the fact that the perfect will of the Father would be accomplished, Peter notwithstanding.

There is a sequel to this episode that John doesn't record. Doctor Luke in his Gospel tells us that Divine surgery was performed at the last minute, rendered necessary by Peter's rushing to the defense of Jesus. This was the last miracle of bodily cure that Jesus wrought. And to think it was on the High Priest's servant! Jesus simply touched the man's ear, and it was instantaneously healed. One would think that the men standing around would have dropped their weapons in amazement and fallen at the feet of this one who, in the face of death, was doing good to those who were despitefully using him.

I have to ask myself, How busy do I keep the Lord as he goes around healing wounds that I've caused on other people? Ironside remarks: "I am sure that Peter would have had great difficulty in leading Malchus to Christ after cutting off his ear! Don't cut people's ears off and then expect them to hear your message." [1] Slashing out, using one's tongue in particular as a weapon, is dangerous business. I think Jesus would say to us today: "Put your sword away!"

The narrative unfolds, and through it all, even as we see the power of Satan and the sin of those who succumb to his wiles, we catch this glimpse of the silent and irresistible movement of the will of God.

THE ACTUAL ARREST

So the Jewish police, with the soldiers and their lieutenant, arrested Jesus and tied him. First they took him to Annas, the father-in-law of Caiaphas, the High Priest that year. Caiaphas was the one who told the other Jewish leaders, "Better that one should die for all" (vss. 12–14).

Jesus was seized and bound as a common criminal. *They* bound *him?* They only thought they bound him! What actually bound him? Love for us.

[1] H. A. Ironside, pp. 786, 787.

This arraignment of Jesus before Annas was a preliminary examination. He stood before these, his judges, who someday will stand before him and his judgment seat and receive an eternal sentence.

PETER'S FIRST DENIAL

Simon Peter followed along behind, as did another of the disciples who was acquainted with the High Priest. So that other disciple was permitted into the courtyard along with Jesus, while Peter stood outside the gate. Then the other disciple spoke to the girl watching at the gate, and she let Peter in. The girl asked Peter, "Aren't you one of Jesus' disciples?"

"No," he said, "I am not!"

The police and the household servants were standing around a fire they had made, for it was cold. And Peter stood there with them, warming himself (vss. 15–18).

Only Peter and John dared to follow Jesus to that house. John, because of some acquaintanceship with the High Priest, was permitted into the courtyard alongside Jesus. Peter is left outside the gate until John whispers to the girl at the gate to let him in.

Peter was running scared, but let's give him credit for at least being there. The others fled running and kept on running, but not Peter and John. Peter was under the influence of very mixed feelings. It is hard to believe that the saucy sarcasm of a little servant-maid should trip him up. Peter wasn't the first man to get himself into trouble just because of a woman —and a woman's curiosity at that. Peter was but the first of many men who have thought it easier to "get off the hook" by lying than to tell the truth to a woman. When will men learn that women aren't that easily deceived? I doubt very much that he fooled this sharp little Miss. He didn't get away with a thing. She correctly sized up the situation. It is always dangerous to warm oneself at the fire of one's enemies. In the final analysis, Peter got burned playing with fire.

JESUS INSIDE WITH THE HIGH PRIEST
BEING INTERROGATED

There was a brief interrogatory before Annas, who was looking for something upon which he could fasten a charge against Jesus. He wanted to bring Jesus within the grip of the government.

Jesus had done nothing in a clandestine way. He had not been underhanded. He answered with dignified boldness. Jesus' courage and unflinching tone is an example to those of us who face the enemies of our Lord. We are to stand our ground, firmly and confidently asserting the truth.

But there was a tone of righteous anger in Jesus' voice as he suggested that Annas ask others who had heard him teach. Annas's line of examination was grossly unjust; he was trying to get Jesus to incriminate himself. The insolence of one of the soldiers stings as we read of Jesus being struck while bound. This was a definite breach of the law. Jesus bore this affront with meekness and patience (vss. 19–24).

PETER'S SECOND AND THIRD DENIAL

Meanwhile, as Simon Peter was standing by the fire, he was asked again, "Aren't you one of his disciples?"

"Of course not," he replied.

But one of the household slaves of the High Priest—a relative of the man whose ear Peter had cut off—asked, "Didn't I see you out there in the olive grove with Jesus?"

Again Peter denied it. And immediately a rooster crowed (vss. 25–27).

Jesus had earlier told Peter that before the cock crowed he would deny him three times. It was just a simple crowing of a cock, but to Peter it must have sounded like a clap of thunder as he recalled what Jesus said, and it awoke in him a profound sense of his sin and his fall.

But Peter's fall was only momentary; it was not his faith

that had failed, only his courage. That can happen to even the strongest of saints. It does not mean that God can no longer use us. Peter went out and wept bitterly. Sorrow over sin will result in tears from the truly contrite heart. Our Father notes each tear that falls; they are precious to him when shed over a recognition of our failure and sin. Peter deeply loved Jesus. Peter was not a Judas. Peter's fall will forever stand as an instructive example of what can happen if we fail to watch and pray, and if we fail to stay close to the Savior. It shows the tender care of our Lord as he extends his hand of mercy and lifts up the fallen, restoring such a one to future service.

Let us not judge this failure of Peter too harshly. God allowed this mercifully for our benefit, to prevent others with a Simon-nature from making shipwreck of their lives. It is a strong beacon light. Pride, self-confidence, prayerlessness, fear of what others may think—these are human weaknesses we all possess to a more or less degree. The same strong hand that saved Peter from drowning on an earlier occasion would once more be stretched out to raise him from his fall in the High Priest's hall. Peter's weakness serves to show Christ's compassion. *Peter, you did not fall in vain, for I know that when my faith wavers, Jesus will do for me what he did for you.*

25

The Silence of Love:
The Model Sufferer

The Text: John 18:28–40; 19:1–16
The Place: Pilate's Palace
The Event: The "Trial" Before Pilate

There could not have been a sympathizing God without a
suffering Savior. Jesus plumbed the depths of human agony
so that he could fully identify with us in all that comes into
our lives. He speaks of his sufferings as a "cup" given to him
by his Father. When Peter wildly slashed out at the High
Priest's servant with his sword, Jesus gently rebuked him:
"Put your sword away. Shall I not drink from the cup the
Father has given me?" (John 18:11). Now that "cup" is
being pressed to his lips—so potent and so bitter.

JESUS BEFORE PILATE

Jesus' trial before Caiaphas ended in the early hours of the
morning. Next he was taken to the palace of the Roman
governor. His accusers wouldn't go in themselves for that
would "defile" them, they said, and they wouldn't be allowed
to eat the Passover lamb. So Pilate, the governor, went out
to them and asked, "What is your charge against this man?
What are you accusing him of doing?" (vss. 28, 29).

When Pilate questioned this troublesome mob of Jews as
to the charge they were bringing against Jesus, they retorted:

161

"We wouldn't have arrested him if he weren't a criminal!"
(vs. 30).

Pilate, as judge, is calling for an indictment.
Their answer shows disdain for him as representative of the
Roman government.

These accusers told Pilate that Jesus was perverting the
nation, leading the people to ruin and telling them not to pay
their taxes to the Roman government; also that he was
claiming to be the Messiah King (Luke 23:2).

It was a trumped-up charge, for these Jewish men well knew
that no Roman court would sentence a man to death merely
on a charge of blasphemy (i.e., declaring himself to be the
Son of God). A domestic religious squabble was insufficient
reason to involve the Roman government. The charge, therefore, that the Jews leveled against Jesus was that he was a
political agitator advocating civil disorder and revolution.

But Pilate did not want to consider the accusation:

> "Take him away and judge him yourselves by your own
> laws," Pilate told them.
> "But we want him crucified," they demanded, "and your
> approval is required." This fulfilled Jesus' prediction con-
> cerning the method of his execution (vss. 31, 32).

Now the truth comes out! But they are less insolent than
before. Pilate is clever. If they are to achieve their desired end,
they must change their tack a bit. Pilate was a cold, dis-
passionate man, but he was not dumb. He hadn't risen to this
position of power through ignorance. He turns his back on
these men whom he holds in such contempt.

THE PRISONER BEFORE THE BAR

Then Pilate went back into the palace and called for Jesus
to be brought to him. "Are you the King of the Jews?" he
asked him (vs. 33).

Pilate has not confronted Jesus before. Now, when he sees him, he does not ask Jesus about his "revolutionary activities" but instead comes right to the point. He knew a political insurrectionist when he saw one, and Jesus obviously did not fit the description of a revolutionary! Pilate was not fooled. He soon discovered that he was face to face with an extraordinary man. Jesus' comment tips him off balance:

> " 'King' as *you* use the word or as the *Jews* use it?" Jesus asked (vs. 34).

It was a tremendously searching question. Who is on trial now? The representative of Roman power was confronted with someone about whom there was a definite air of kingliness. Jesus was majestically calm and in control of the situation as well as of himself.

Quickly Pilate regains his composure:

> "Am I a Jew?" Pilate retorted. "Your own people and their chief priests brought you here. Why? What have you done?" (vs. 35).

The sharp-sighted procurator would like to get out of this miserable situation. He knew this was no case for his tribunal; he knew Jesus was innocent; perjured evidence had put Jesus in this position.

> Then Jesus answered, "I am not an earthly king. If I were, my followers would have fought when I was arrested by the Jewish leaders. But my Kingdom is not of this world" (vs. 36).

Jesus' humble attire and appearance certainly did not bespeak kingship. But Pilate was aware of the rumor prevalent throughout the East at that time, that a king was about to rise among the Jews. I would imagine at that point Pilate had an uncomfortable, frightened awareness creep over him that he was in the presence of a most uncommon man; there was an unearthly quality about him. And the man did claim to have a kingdom!

Pilate replied, "But you are a king then?"

"Yes," Jesus said. "I was born for that purpose. And I came to bring truth to the world. All who love the truth are my followers" (vs. 37).

Barnhouse observes that this was Christ's announcement of the purpose of Christmas. Christmas in Pilate's judgment hall approximately six or eight hours before he was crucified! The Apostle Paul in writing to Timothy explained that Jesus "witnessed a good confession" before Pilate.

THE AGE-OLD QUESTION OF THE SKEPTIC

Jesus cared even about Pilate. Pilate was a man who needed a Savior. Jesus was offering Pilate an opportunity to hear words of truth.

"What is truth?" Pilate exclaimed (vs. 38a).

But Pilate didn't wait for an answer. Pilate heard Jesus' voice in his ear, but he did not listen to that voice in his heart. He spoke as a worldly minded Roman noble, a man who had listened to much philosophical speculation about such matters as truth. He shrugs his shoulders, cynically asks the question, and then walks away from the Truth.

THE VERDICT PRONOUNCED

Then he (Pilate) went out again to the people and told them, "He is not guilty of any crime. But you have a custom of asking me to release someone from prison each year at Passover. So if you want me to, I'll release the 'King of the Jews'" (vss. 38b, 39).

This was the official sentence of a Roman judge. It was acquittal. "Not guilty" would be what a judge would say today and slam down his gavel.

Pilate offered the people a choice between release of Barabbas or Jesus. The reputation of Barabbas was commonly known—he was a robber, an insurrectionist, and a murderer. It was an appallingly wicked thing that Pilate did. If Pilate had possessed the honesty and courage that become a judge, he would have discharged Jesus.

It has been suggested that Pilate actually thought the people's voice would rise louder than that of those who had brought Jesus to him. Five days before, "the whole world," using the language of the enemies of Jesus, had applauded Jesus; Pilate felt that they would not now turn against Jesus. It was a desperate attempt to escape his responsibility with respect to Jesus. His strategy failed, for the Hosanna-shouters either failed to put in an appearance at this early-morning trial or else they were out-shouted by Jesus' enemies.

> But they screamed back, "No! Not this man, but Barabbas!" (vs. 40).

JESUS SCOURGED, CROWNED WITH THORNS, AND BEATEN

The implacable hostility of the Jews would not be appeased by this strategy. Never was there such an exhibition of the depth of human wickedness. Pilate was convinced that the prisoner before him was innocent and that he ought to acquit him, yet he feared the Jewish people and popular opinion. In his double-mindedness he supposed that by scourging Jesus in the Roman fashion—which was unspeakably cruel—the people would be satisfied, and that after seeing Jesus beaten, bleeding, and torn with rods, they would be content to let him go.

> Then Pilate laid open Jesus' back with a leaded whip, and the soldiers made a crown of thorns and placed it on his head and robed him in royal purple. "Hail, 'King of the Jews!" they mocked, and struck him with their fists (John 19:1–3).

Pilate violated all justice in having Jesus scourged, but this was a last-ditch effort to appease these bloodthirsty Jews. It was a weak design and did not move the enemies of Jesus a fraction of an inch in their irreconcilable hatred of him and their grim determination to see him die.

The flagellation was followed by a mock coronation. Pilate turned Jesus over to the soldiers, who made sport of him and, with fiendish cruelty, pressed down a "crown" that they had fastened together of thorny twigs. Jesus, the innocent sin-bearer, wore this crown of thorns so that we, the guilty ones, might someday wear a crown of glory. The mock royal robe of purple was another mark of contempt and derision designed to show how contemptible and ridiculous was the idea of his having a kingdom. Our wonderful Savior was clothed with this ugly robe of shame so that you and I might be clothed with a spotless robe of righteousness before the throne of God. This was all a part of the "cup" that Jesus was "drinking" for our sakes.

The scourging and mockery now completed, the Roman governor once more goes forth from the palace to the Jews waiting outside:

"I am going to bring him out to you now, but understand that I find him *not guilty*" (vs. 4).

PILATE'S FINAL EFFORTS TO RELEASE JESUS

Clearly Pilate's tack is to work on the sympathy of the people. As he exposes to their view this pathetic spectacle covered with wounds, blood streaking down his face, neck, arms, and back, the horrible crown pressed down upon his forehead, the robe hanging awkwardly, Jesus presents a pitiful sight. But Pilate did not reckon with the hardness of the sinful human heart and its capacity for hatred. The sight that he hoped would arouse their pity and satisfy them only called forth their lust for revenge.

Then Jesus came out wearing the crown of thorns and the purple robe. And Pilate said, "Behold the man!" (vs. 5).

This was *the caring Jesus*. The dramatic appeal was ended and without effect.

JEWISH FANATICISM AND ROMAN JUSTICE CLASH

Palestine was a notoriously explosive province, and right from the beginning of his term of office Pilate was in trouble with the Jews. They were stubborn and inflexible; there were many clashes in the contest of wills. The Romans were surprisingly tolerant through much of this, though Pilate's personal corruption, his acts of insolence, his habit of insulting people, his murder of people untried, and his inhumanity were common knowledge. Now once again Pilate is engaged in a bitter wrestling match with these proud and resolute religious leaders. It is Jewish fanaticism and Roman justice clashing.

Never underestimate the power of a woman. Part of Pilate's hesitation to bow to the will of these Jews was the fact that his wife had sent word to him that she'd had a vivid dream that was a warning: "Leave that good man alone; for I had a terrible nightmare concerning him last night" (Matt. 27:19). His wife's words rose up before him as he faced that howling mob of Jews whose leaders, half-crazed with hate and envy, led in shouting,

"Crucify! Crucify!" (vs. 6).

The peoples' emotions were out of control; but Pilate is the picture of frustration. He has been described as an animal caught in a trap, twisting and turning and unable to find any way of escape. "Never was any governor less capable of governing, or any ruler more tragically helpless." [1]

But the picture I want to arrest the reader's attention is that of Jesus. Can you see him? He was the supreme example of serenity in the face of sin and injustice the likes of which has never since been equaled. Jesus had the calm serenity that comes from knowing you are standing in the will of God. That same assurance can be ours in *every* time of testing.

[1] William Barclay, *The Mind of Jesus* (New York: Harper & Row, 1960), p. 238.

Pilate was still unwilling to concede to the clamor of the mob.

> "*You* crucify him," Pilate said. "I find him *not guilty*" (vs. 6b).

Matthew Henry points out that the guards of governors ought to be the guards of justice. Pilate's power was supposed to be used to protect the innocent and injured. But in the end, Pilate capitulates to blackmail.

> They replied, "By our laws he ought to die because he called himself the Son of God."
> When Pilate heard this, he was more frightened than ever. He took Jesus back into the palace again and asked him, "Where are you from?" but Jesus gave no answer (vss. 7–9).

This new charge of blasphemy against Jesus frightened Pilate. His wife's dream came sharply into focus: What if he actually did have before him some God in human form! The thought terrified him.

> "You won't talk to me?" Pilate demanded. "Don't you realize that I have the power to release you or to crucify you?"
> Then Jesus said, "You would have no power at all over me unless it were given to you from above. So those who brought me to you have the greater sin" (vss. 10, 11).

Pilate again was impressed with Jesus' answer and attitude. This Man even had regard for his authority! Once more he intensified his efforts to release Jesus.

> Then Pilate tried to release him, but the Jewish leaders told him, "If you release this man, you are no friend of Caesar's. Anyone who declares himself a king is a rebel against Caesar" (vs. 12).

PILATE IS FLOORED

It was the final straw and a clever one. It weighed heavily on the mind of this weak Roman governor. He trampled on his conscience to avoid the wrath of an earthly monarch.

At these words Pilate brought Jesus out to them again and sat down at the judgment bench on the stone-paved platform. It was now about noon of the day before Passover.
And Pilate said to the Jews, "Here is your king!"
"Away with him," they yelled. "Away with him—crucify him!"
"What? Crucify your king?" Pilate asked.
"We have no king but Caesar," the chief priests shouted back" (vss. 13–15).

When Pilate saw that he was gaining nothing but that riot was beginning instead, he took some water and washed his hands in the presence of the crowd and said, "I am innocent of the blood of this good man. The responsibility is yours!"

And the mob yelled back, "His blood be on us and on our children!" (Matt. 27:24, 25).

THE CASE IS CLOSED

Then Pilate gave Jesus to them to be crucified (vs. 16).

The Jewish nation, through their rulers, and Pilate, bowed the neck to Caesar in order to murder Jesus. Christ was delivered to death, that you and I might be delivered from death and the bondage of sin.

26

Mankind's Darkest Hour:
The Uplifted Savior

The Text: John 19:17–30
The Place: Golgotha, Outside the City of Jerusalem
The Event: The Crucifixion

Jesus' crucifixion is God's pledge that my sins, which were many, have been dealt with and that they no longer stand in the way of my relationship with the Father.

I cannot read the Gospel accounts of Christ's crucifixion, without hearing the thud of the soldiers' hammers nailing Jesus to that horrible cross and thinking about something the Apostle Paul said: "God took my sins and nailed them to Christ's cross."

John, with reverent reticence, tells the events of the hours on the cross.

THEY CRUCIFIED HIM

So they had him at last, and he was taken out of the city, carrying his cross to the place known as "The Skull," in Hebrew, "Golgotha." There they crucified him and two others with him, one on either side, with Jesus between them. And Pilate posted a sign over him reading, "Jesus of Nazareth, the King of the Jews." The place where Jesus was crucified was near the city; and the signboard was written in Hebrew, Latin, and Greek, so that many people read it.

Then the chief priests said to Pilate, "Change it from 'The

King of the Jews' to '*He said*, I am King of the Jews.' "
Pilate replied, "What I have written, I have written. It
stays exactly as it is" (John 19:17–22).

Great crowds trailed along behind, and many grief-stricken
women. Jesus had a word for them:

"Daughters of Jerusalem, don't weep for me, but for yourselves and for your children" (Luke 23:28).

It was said in ancient times that the person who was crucified "died a thousand deaths." It was the kind of death that
combined the maximum of pain with the least immediate
destruction of life.

Jesus was crucified in between two thieves. This was done
deliberately, to show preeminence in guilt. It was an act of
malice by his enemies, but God meant it for good (for as the
world's Savior, he had taken upon himself the sin of the
world; he was made to be the chiefest of sinners).

God in his wonderful providence directed the hand of Pilate
as he wrote the superscription that went up over the head of
Christ. Golgotha was near the city, and the pilgrims thronging
into Jerusalem from many parts of the world read what was
written in their own language. He was the uplifted Savior, the
King of the Jews, and Pilate unwittingly provided a Witness
for all the world. Of course the Jewish leaders took offense at
this—as far as they were concerned, Jesus was *not* their national Messiah. The Jewish dignitaries demanded that the
governor change the wording from "The King of the Jews" to
"*He said,* I am King of the Jews." But Pilate doggedly de-
clined. In this he achieved at least a minor victory as he stands
his ground declaring: "What I have written, I have written. It
stays exactly as it is."

THE WOMEN AT THE CROSS

Never let it be said that women don't possess courage!
Don't let anyone scoff at the supposed cowardice and weak-

ness of women. The weaker sex, we are called. Is that true? From what we can tell, all but one of Jesus' disciples forsook him at the cross, but there was more than one woman who boldly confessed him by staying near him. Women were the last to leave the cross, and they were the first to arrive at the tomb.

> Standing near the cross were Jesus' mother, Mary, his aunt, the wife of Cleopas, and Mary Magdalene (vs. 25).

Jesus was a condemned man being executed by Roman soldiers not especially known for being gentle and considerate. You can be sure there was a taunting crowd of Jews and rough people standing about (that type of people are always attracted to something of this nature). These women are to be tremendously admired for the faithfulness and courage they displayed in the face of such hatred. The vulgarity of these men and the language they undoubtedly used did not deter these women one bit from standing by.

The sight of their beloved Jesus hanging on the cross, blood-spattered and struggling for breath, would have been enough to unnerve and shock even the toughest of men. The crowd gaped and jeered. The Jewish leaders laughed and scoffed. The soldiers mocked him. But the women, though torn with anguish, remained self-controlled, calm, and constant. They did not faint, nor did they go into hysterics. Not all women could have done this; not all women today can go through such trauma. But these women did demonstrate deep affection and an amazing degree of emotional stability that had its roots in the strength that God was supplying.

It has been my privilege in years' past to interview and spend time with women whom I refer to as "cameos" and "silhouettes" in two other books.[1] Also, as I have spoken and traveled across the country and into Canada, I have met women who know the meaning of freedom in Christ, which satisfies as nothing else can. These women have not par-

---

[1] *Cameos, Women Fashioned by God* (Wheaton, Ill.: Tyndale House Publishers, 1968), *Silhouettes, Women Behind Great Men* (Waco, Tex.: Word Books, 1972).

ticipated in demonstrations calling for equality, nor have they kicked up their heels in protest calling for a redefinement of the role of women in society. There is no need for this on the part of the woman who recognizes her worth in the eyes of Jesus.

Throughout Jesus' earthly ministry women were regularly on hand, participating in his work, learning as well as serving, absorbing his teachings and fellowship. It was a male-run world, but Jesus included women and for all time lifted their status. The Jewish scholar Joachim Jeremias says that this was "an unprecedented happening in the history of that time."

Jesus treated women as full-fledged persons rather than reducing them to a sex-based caste of usable bodies and mealtime menials. It made him an especially magnetic personality to women. Their respect and love for Jesus showed as they risked all in his final crucial hours. They were steadfast, unwavering allies.

I see women like that today, women who have been loosed from the grip of sin that bound them into being something less than what God intended them to be. These women possess an inner peace and beauty that radiantly sets them apart. They are the kind of woman who, if they had lived in Jesus' time, would have been a part of that loyal group at the cross.

The Apostle Paul wrote: "There is neither Jew nor Greek, there is neither slave nor free, there is neither male nor female, for you are all one in Christ Jesus." This kind of teaching would have had to come from Jesus and be passed down to Paul.

JESUS' PROVISION FOR HIS MOTHER FROM THE CROSS

When Jesus therefore saw his mother, and the disciple whom he loved standing nearby, he said to his mother, "Woman, behold, your son!"

Then he said to the disciple, "Behold, your mother!" And from that hour the disciple took her into his own household (vss. 26, 27 NAS).

Even in the midst of his great pain, when Jesus' eyes fell upon his Mother standing there with John, his heart went out to her as he forgot his own bodily and mental agony.

As Jesus' eyes fell upon the face that had first looked into his when he came into the world, when he looked at the one who had so tenderly cared for him and nurtured him as an infant and youth, he made provision for her for the rest of her earthly life. He loved the disciple John and knew him to be trustworthy; there was no better way to provide for his mother than to put her into the care of this dear friend.

MARY'S SWORD AND HER SON'S CROSS

And what of Mary? What emotions surged through her being? Only women can really understand the emotions of another woman. The full cycle of what we, as mothers, experience with our children is something known peculiarly to us alone. Mary was all pain. In those long, tormented moments as she and the others waited at the foot of the cross, watching the precious life blood drain out of Jesus, she experienced what old Simeon, a devout man filled with the Holy Spirit, had prophesied at the time of Jesus' presentation as an infant in the Temple: "A sword shall pierce your soul, for this child shall be rejected by many in Israel, and this to their undoing. But he will be the greatest joy of many others. And the deepest thoughts of many hearts shall be revealed" (Luke 2:28–35).

Now, Mary stood silently, with that beautiful composure that comes in the time of deepest grief when you are held and sustained by the inner power that comes from God. To herself she silently said, "My Son, my Son. God's Son, God's Son." With that came blessed release for this precious mother.

No woman's pain was ever more complete than Mary's, but she took God's strength to move her attention away from her own anguish toward the anguish of the one she loved above every other person on earth. This is possible for us, if it was possible for her. Her Son has hung on his cross now, and we can know in retrospect, that power enough was released that dark day, to move us away from our own pain into a creative action toward our own loved ones.

Pain is still pain, but God is still God. We only need to be willing, as Mary was willing, to look away from our pain toward love. And once we look, he will give us the inner power to act on what we see.[2]

There has been much misunderstanding about Jesus' use of the word *woman* in addressing his mother. Hendriksen's explanation has cleared this up for me:

> It was very kind of Jesus to say, "Woman," and not, "Mother." The word "Mother" would have driven the sword even more deeply into the soul of Mary, that sharp and painful sword of which Simeon had spoken. Here at the cross, exactly as at Cana's wedding it was very kind of Jesus to emphasize by the use of the word *woman* that Mary must no longer think of him as being merely her son; for, the more she conceives of him as her son, the more also will she suffer when he suffers. Mary must begin to look upon Jesus as her *Lord*. Yes, even then she will suffer, but this suffering will be of a different nature. She will then know that though indescribably terrible, his agony is, nevertheless, glorious because of its purpose. She will then begin to concentrate on its redemptive meaning. Hence, not *mother* but *woman*. Mary's emotional suffering—as any mother would suffer for her son who was being crucified—must be replaced by something higher and nobler, that is, by adoration!"[3]

THE ACCOMPLISHMENT

The last dregs of the "cup" were being taken by our blessed Lord. John quietly passes over some of the next movements in this Divine tragedy as it moves to its climax. When the sun was in its zenith, instead of the brightness of noon, darkness fell across the whole land for three hours. Midnight darkness at noontide would be frightening.

[2] Eugenia Price, *God Speaks to Women Today* (Grand Rapids, Mich.: Zondervan Publishing House, 1964), p. 168.
[3] William Hendriksen, *The Gospel of John*, p. 433.

Up until this time not one word had escaped from the lips of Jesus showing his human agony. Not until all things were accomplished did he give vent to his pent-up suffering.

> After this, Jesus, knowing that all things had already been accomplished, in order that the Scripture might be fulfilled, said, "I am thirsty" (vs. 28 NAS).

But there was more to it than human thirst. Jesus thirsted after the glorifying of God; he could never have been satisfied with his mission to earth if he had not accomplished the Father's will. Isaiah 53, in speaking of the scandal of the cross and the benefits of Christ's passion, says that "As a result of the anguish of his soul, he will see it and be satisfied" (vs. 11).

> A jar of sour wine was sitting there, so a sponge was soaked in it and put on a hyssop branch and held up to his lips (vs. 29).

THE GLORIOUS CONSUMMATION

> When Jesus had tasted it, he said, "It is finished," and bowed his head and dismissed his spirit (vs. 30).

The last of the "cup" was taken. What was finished? The atonement for sin and the bringing in of everlasting assurance of salvation to all who believe. Our redemption was complete. "It is finished" was a word of triumph at the glorious consummation of his mission to earth.

Jesus, whom John so beautifully describes as the Light of the world, was now dead, his enemies could say. The Light was at last extinguished. Was it?

> "Lord, bend that proud and stiffnecked I,
>   Help me to bow the head and die;
> Beholding him on Calvary,
>   Who bowed his head for me." [4]

[4] Roy Hession, *The Calvary Road* (Fort Washington, Pa.: Christian Literature Crusade, 1950), p. 15.

27

Aftermath of the Cross:
He Died and Was Buried

The Text: John 19:31–42
The Place: A Garden Near the Place of the Crucifixion
The Event: Jesus' Burial

Life ended. Hope, for many, was gone. The "cup" had been drained to the dregs by Crowned Sorrow. Light had first been eclipsed and then extinguished, Love eliminated. This was the dead Jesus. Was there to be no more life? No more hope? No more Light? No more love? If John's Gospel had ended with these eleven verses (John 19:31–42), we would have had to answer yes to such questions. But praise God! there is more! Much more! Out of that awful, abysmal darkness immediately following Jesus' dismissing of his Spirit (death), the great Light that lights the world was once again to flame.

> Eternal life is in him, and this life gives light to all mankind. His life is the light that shines through the darkness— and the darkness can never extinguish it (John 1:4, 5).

Jesus' enemies were certain they had put out the Light. He died that day, to be sure, and he was buried, and it appeared that the dark, evil deeds of malicious men had triumphed. But heaven was watching. It was sometime after three o'clock on Friday afternoon.

The Jewish leaders didn't want the victims hanging there the next day, which was the Sabbath (and a very special Sabbath at that, for it was the Passover), so they asked Pilate to order the legs of the men broken to hasten death; then their bodies could be taken down. So the soldiers came and broke the legs of the two men crucified with Jesus; but when they came to him, they saw that he was dead already, so they didn't break his. However, one of the soldiers pierced his side with a spear, and blood and water flowed out. I saw all this myself and have given an accurate report so that you can believe. The soldiers did this in fulfillment of the Scripture that says, "Not one of his bones shall be broken," and, "They shall look on him whom they pierced" (vs. 31–37).

What does the soldier desire after a long and hard battle? Peace. What does the worker seek after bitter toil? Rest. And what does the heart and body crave after agony? Ease.

Jesus was only thirty-three when he died. That life was a battle for Jesus after he began his public ministry cannot be denied. That he knew what it was to put in an honest day's toil is a recognized fact. The demands upon his person were great. There was very little rest and ease for him so long as he was in the presence of need. He wept when others wept; he hurt when others hurt. In *all* respects, he was a caring Jesus.

But now we see our uplifted Savior, hanging on the cross, head bowed in death. The weight of the sin of the world was heavy upon him. The soldier at peace. The battle ended. The workman at rest. His labor finished. The heart and body at ease. Quiet in death. His Spirit with the Father.

We see the Jewish religious leaders requesting the removal of the dead bodies. By all means the ritual of religion must be observed (it did not matter that its principles were violated).

Jesus, in talking to the Jewish leaders at the outset of his public ministry, made this claim (which they did not understand): "Destroy this temple, and in three days I will raise it up" (John 2:19 AV). If Jesus had been left to hang on the cross, as was the Roman custom (leaving the bodies there to putrefy), he could not have fulfilled that prophecy and risen the third day after his death.

But notice how God uses Jesus' enemies as tools in his hand to accomplish his purpose. The Jews interfered in the affairs of the Romans and got Pilate to give consent to removal of the bodies (vs. 31). It was the enemies of Jesus who paved the way for the crowning miracle of Jesus' resurrection!

The soldiers came, under Pilate's orders, to break the legs of the malefactors, thus hastening their death. The bones were literally pounded to pieces with heavy blows from a hammer or iron or some available instrument. A medical doctor says that shock attending such cruel injury to bones can be the coup de grace causing death. Mercifully, Jesus was spared this additional agony, for he was already dead. The Roman soldiers were accustomed to making sure the victim was dead before removal from the cross; therefore, we are told that it was they who confirmed the fact and gave witness to Jesus' actual death (vs. 33).

But there was a second proof that he was dead. One of the soldiers pierced Jesus' side with his spear and "blood and water flowed out" (vs. 34). The spear did not put Jesus to death; he was dead already.

The physiological explanation of this quite generally accepted (particularly by physicians and specialists) as the ruptured-heart theory. But who can doubt that even the soldier's spear was guided by a loving Father's hand. John is not interested primarily in the physiology of this spectacle of blood and water, but he calls attention to it because of its greater spiritual significance.

Blood and water were used under the Law. To the devout Jew this was highly significant—blood for atonement, water for purification. There is benefit for the believer in the blood and water that flowed from Christ's side. We are assured of life and spiritual health because the Life-giver poured himself out for us.

Who can doubt that this was God's answer to humanity's sin! Do not regard that spear thrust too lightly, for it was bathed with blood, evidence of the compassionate heart of the caring Jesus.

John states that all of this happened in fulfillment of the

Scripture (vs. 37). To what is John referring? In Exodus 12 instructions are given as to the sacrifice of the paschal lamb: it was to be perfect, and no bone of it was to be broken (Ex. 12:46). When Jesus first came on the scene, John the Baptist announced him by saying, "Behold, the Lamb of God, which taketh away the sin of the world" (John 1:29). Jesus was the true paschal Lamb, and no bone of him was broken.

John remembered also that in the book of Zechariah it says, "They shall look upon him whom they have pierced" (Zech. 12:10). Jesus' side was pierced and the prophetic foretelling fulfilled.

JESUS' BODY IN THE HANDS OF THOSE WHO LOVED HIM

Not only did Jesus' enemies go to Pilate and make a request about the men hanging on the crosses, but one of Jesus' secret disciples did a very bold thing. John relates the incident:

> Afterwards Joseph of Arimathea, who had been a secret disciple of Jesus for fear of the Jewish leaders, boldly asked Pilate for permission to take Jesus' body down; and Pilate told him to go ahead. So he came and took it away (vs. 38).

But Joseph had help. He acted in concert with Nicodemus (vss. 39–40).

Both men are criticized by some commentators for their secrecy in being Jesus' disciples. This is looked upon as weakness and sinful fear. Others regard them as hidden servants, yes, but honorable and well-known to God. Not all of God's saints are as bold as Peter was in the garden, yet they love Christ and are loved by him. Where was Peter now and the other disciples when it was time to do something about the body of Jesus?

Christ's suffering had a mighty effect on Joseph and Nicodemus. They would suffer the consequences at the hands of their Jewish cohorts. Nothing mattered now but to take care of that mutilated body of this one they loved. Circumstances can bring out character in extraordinary ways. What these two men did was the last ministry of love for Jesus. Already we see the wonderful power of Christ's death in these who now possess not only courage, but strong love.

THE BURIAL OF THE KING

The place of crucifixion was near a grove of trees, where there was a new tomb, never used before. And so, because of the need for haste before the Sabbath, and because the tomb was close at hand, they laid him there (vss. 41, 42).

Over-ruling Providence provided a nearby tomb that was new. God took care of all the final details for his Son. It was a tomb fit for a king! Without pomp or ceremony, the King is buried.

PART V

Victor Over Death

28

Dawn of Victory:
He Is Alive Again!

The Text: John 20:1–18
The Place: The Empty Tomb in the Garden
The Event: The Resurrection

The corpse of Friday night arose again a living man on Sunday morning! But how could a man who couldn't even ward the flies from off his face as he hung helpless on a cross be the power of God? How utter defeat can miraculously be turned to triumphant victory is the glowing truth of Christianity.

The resurrection of Christ from the dead is the most important fact in the whole fund of human knowledge that has ever been amassed. There is *nothing* that can equal it. It is *the* grand event of the ages, toward which all previous history moved, and in which all subsequent history finds its meaning.

Radical critics of the resurrection have gone to great lengths to disprove the appearances of Christ. But the one thing they cannot explain away is the existence of the Christian Church down through the centuries.

It is beyond dispute that the existence of the Church is due to the conviction of the disciples that Jesus had risen from the dead. It would be very difficult to believe that the beginning of the Church and the continued existence of the Church are based either on an hallucination or on an im-

185

posture. In view of the existence of the Church it is more difficult not to believe in the Resurrection than it is to believe in it. . .

It is impossible to think of the whole of Christianity being founded on a lie. It is impossible to think of the disciples preaching the Resurrection faith and dying for the Resurrection faith in the full awareness that the whole thing was a deliberate falsehood. As Joseph Klausner, himself a great Jew and scholar, says: "That is impossible; *deliberate imposture* is not the substance out of which the religion of millions of mankind is created . . . The nineteen hundred years' faith of millions is not founded on deception." [1]

The hopes of Jesus' disciples had been dashed to pieces. They fled in terror, understandably fearful that they, too, might suffer the same tragic fate as Jesus. But there were those who could not abandon their beloved friend to the tomb, among them a devoted group of women. The other Gospels tell us that Mary Magdalene did not come alone. John says, however, that

> Early Sunday morning, while it was still dark, Mary Magdalene came to the tomb and found that the stone was rolled aside from the entrance (John 20:1).

She Loved Him Much

Love drew those women to the tomb; but Mary's love stands out preeminently and for good reason. Mary was a woman who could not forget. Mary's gratitude showed itself in endless devotion to Christ while he was living, and now in death. Much had been forgiven her, therefore she loved much. She was possessed by seven demons at one time, and Jesus cast them all out. To be healed from such a severe mental sickness would surely call forth one's eternal gratitude. Of all the grateful women in the Bible, Mary Magdalene is the outstanding person.

[1] William Barclay, *The Mind of Jesus*, pp. 294, 295, 306, 307.

MARY MAKES THE GREAT DISCOVERY

Charles R. Erdman makes the observation that it is the mourner who stands weeping at the grave of buried hopes who, perhaps first of all, needs the vision of a risen Christ.[2] Mary came weeping to the grave. How brave she was! I'm not so sure I would have dared venture forth in the darkness of the early morning hours, and to a grave at that! The Passover Feast had just been celebrated, and there were many strangers sleeping along the way. Either Mary came alone, agreeing to meet the other women at the tomb, or, if they came together, Mary was leading the way. Mark tells us that "On the way they were discussing how they could ever roll aside the huge stone from the entrance" (Mark 16:3). Faith such as these women possessed, does not take into account the obstacles in the way but moves confidently along the path of love and duty.

DAWN OF VICTORY!

"Surprising comforts are the frequent encouragement of early seekers."[3] It was the dawn of victory, the beginning of a glorious discovery: the Lord was risen; but Mary did not at first understand:

> She ran and found Simon Peter and me and said, "They have taken the Lord's body out of the tomb, and I don't know where they have put him!" (vs. 2).

In terrified distress, Mary ran off to seek Peter and John. Despair reigns supreme as she relates her staggering experience.

Notice where Peter was! With John. The last look we had of Peter was of a man with a broken heart, going out, having

---

[2] Charles R. Erdman, *Gospel of John*, p. 167.
[3] Matthew Henry, *Matthew Henry's Commentary, Vol. V*, p. 1208.

denied our blessed Lord. All praise to John for taking him in during this black time in his life. I dare not pursue the sequence of events without pausing here to point out John's love and tender charity toward his fallen brother. How many contemporary Christians would have done that! The sure mark of a Church where Christ is exalted, is that its people care. Following Jesus' example, John cared about Peter. I fear that far too many would have excommunicated Peter, and are doing so today to the likes of him.

Mary's mournful announcement sent Peter and John flying into action! There was anxiety, perplexity, and excitement. A vast quantity of thoughts must have raced through their minds as they raced with their legs to the tomb. John outdistanced Peter, which gives much warrant for the commonly held belief that he was younger than Peter.

Notice, however, the difference in temperament of the two men: John cautiously stoops down and looks in, Peter rushes up behind and with his usual boldness goes in and sees. Though John could outrun Peter, Peter could outdare John. Peter's willingness to venture into the tomb gave John the needed strength to enter in and see for himself. The result issued forth in belief (vss. 3–9)!

John reconstructs the events, giving significant details as proof of the fact that Christ arose. The description of the graveclothes indicated that the collapsed linen lay wound just where the body had been. It all suggests careful scrutiny, the clothes lying still in their original folds, not unwound, minus Jesus' resurrected body. Everything was orderly. At that moment light dawned. The Light of the world had risen. Living faith embraced the truth of the resurrection as both men recognized the fulfillment of Scripture prophecy.

THE CROWNING REVELATION AND THE DIVINE MANDATE

The climax has been reached, and the two disciples hurry away.

We went on home, and by that time Mary had returned to
the tomb and was standing outside crying. And as she wept,
she stooped and looked in and saw two white-robed angels
sitting at the head and foot of the place where the body of
Jesus had been lying.
  "Why are you crying?" the angels asked her.
  "Because they have taken away my Lord," she replied,
"and I don't know where they have put him."
  She glanced over her shoulder and saw someone standing
behind her. It was Jesus, but she didn't recognize him! "Why
are you crying?" he asked her. "Whom are you looking for?"
She thought he was the gardener.
  "Sir," she said, "if you have taken him away, tell me
where you have put him, and I will go and get him."
  "Mary!" Jesus said. She turned toward him.
  "Master!" she exclaimed.
  "Don't touch me," he cautioned, "for I haven't yet ascended to the Father. But go and find my brothers and tell
them that I ascend to my Father and your Father, my God
and your God."
  Mary Magdalene found the disciples and told them, "I
have seen the Lord!" Then she gave them his message (vss.
10–18).

Tears weren't just trickling down Mary's face; it was unrestrained sobbing as she stood outside the tomb alone in her
aloneness. Tears flowed afresh as she recalled all that Jesus
had done for her. She could never forget, no, never. Her tears
testify eloquently to the power of Jesus when once he is given
admittance to the human heart.
  Mary could not leave until the mystery of the opened tomb
and the missing body was solved. Where there is such love
for Christ, there will always be an accompanying adherence
to him. As she wept she remembered his bitter "cup" of
suffering. But her weeping did not prevent her from stooping
and looking into the tomb. Does that sound familiar to my
women readers? How often haven't you repeatedly looked and
looked, refusing to give up but still seeking in the last place
you left it something that now seems to have vanished! That

is the nature of women. No wonder Christ chose to reveal himself to one of us. Jesus will always honor the strength of love like this.

THOSE WHO HONOR CHRIST WILL BE HONORED BY CHRIST

If Mary had found the grave full, there would have been great cause for weeping, for then Christ would have been dead still, and there would have been no resurrection. I wonder if we can see ourselves in Mary's anxious weeping. So often we mourn over events and things that in reality are within our grasp. What we need is more faith and patience, more time for the full development of God's purposes to be worked out in our lives. It is said that two-thirds of the things we fear in life never happen at all, and two-thirds of the tears we shed are consequently thrown away and shed in vain. Can we believe that all things are working together for our good, for our peace and joy, even though at the moment it seems to be nothing but bitterness, disappointment, and sorrow?

In the curiously different temperaments of men and women Mary responded with her heart. Ryle observes that the head of a woman is generally weaker than that of a man, but the affections are generally stronger. "I think Mary's case teaches us that heart is of more value in God's sight than intellect. Those who feel most and love most get most privileges. The more we love, the more we are like to Christ." [4]

The appearance of the two angels in the tomb did not seem to frighten Mary. Excessive grief can have a very absorbing and stupefying effect on the mind, and I believe she was so swallowed up in her thoughts that these two ministering spirits did not terrify her.

SORROW TURNED TO JOY

Jesus asked Mary the same question the angels had voiced. Her eyes were blurred with tears, but more than that, her eyes

[4] J. C. Ryle, *Ryle's Expository Thoughts on the Gospels*, p. 639.

were holden supernaturally so that she did not distinguish that it was Jesus standing there. His risen body was different, yet not so different that she didn't soon thereafter recognize him, nor that his disciples also didn't later know him. She thought him to be the gardener and said, "Sir, if you have taken him away, tell me where you have put him, and I will go and get him."

This was the splendid language of loyal love, says Morgan. She may have been a strong and healthy woman, but hardly equal to carrying a dead man. But love is capable of doing difficult things.[5]

Recognition came when he uttered one word: her name! It was enough! Her eyes were opened, the truth shone in upon her: her Savior was not dead but alive. The dazzling splendor of the angels did not fill the gap in Mary's heart, but the voice of Jesus, calling her by name, awakened every fiber of her being, and she responded, "Rabboni!"

"My Master," is what Mary was saying. She dropped to her knees in worshipful adoration. Jesus cautioned her against touching him, and she obeyed. Love is always prompt to obey. For too long she had been greatly concerned about his humanity; now Jesus is gently telling her that her Master was God as well as man. Jesus would not have Mary dote upon his bodily presence, and so in tender thoughtfulness and kindness he diverts her thoughts as he summons her not to spend time in demonstrating her affection for him, but to serve him. What an honor! To be commissioned by the Lord himself to carry the good news of his resurrection to others!

This was the first day of the week, but it was also the first day of the rest of Mary's life, and from that moment life took on a new meaning. Perhaps someone reading this has come into a fresh realization of what it means to stand in resurrection Light. Mary was the first witness of Jesus' resurrection, the first to see him, the first to hear his voice, the first to hold conversation with him. The true mark of a disciple of Christ, man or woman, child or youth, is that they are willing and anxious to share the "good news" of Jesus' resur-

[5] G. Campbell Morgan, *The Gospel According to John*, p. 313.

rection. This Mary did. "She was the first herald of the era of grace, of the church, of missions, of world evangelism, of an ascended and glorified Christ, who had entered upon the throne of his spiritual kingdom. She announced first what has called forth our highest devotion and service ever since." [6]

The "central, heartbeat happening of the faith" was first made known to Mary, and through her, proclaimed to others.

[6] Harold J. Ockenga, *Women Who Made Bible History* (Grand Rapids, Mich.: Zondervan Publishing House, 1962), pp. 209, 210.

29

From Everlasting to Everlasting:
The Living Lord!

The Text: John 20:19–31
The Place: Behind Locked Doors Somewhere in Jerusalem or Galilee
The Event: Post-Resurrection Appearances of Jesus

The Resurrection is the star in the firmament of Christianity.

Every effect must have an adequate cause. What can explain the astonishing change in the disciples that we read about in the book of Acts, for instance, and in Peter's writings? After the crucifixion we saw a group of hopeless, disappointed, frightened men fleeing for their lives, with but one desire—to escape back to Galilee. Fear and despair drove these terrified men to flight. This was their condition at Passover; but seven weeks later Pentecost came, and we see these same men emerge filled with blazing hope and courage.

What happened? It was the realization that Jesus had risen from the dead. This conviction came as a result of Jesus' appearance to the disciples and others in his post-resurrection days on earth.

THE APPEARANCE TO TEN DISCIPLES

If anyone has shown us the need to be quick to forgive and forget, it is Jesus. It was Mary Magdalene whom Jesus commissioned to be the apostle to the Apostles. Ryle observes that to trust deserters and to show confidence in backsliders is something we as mere men can hardly understand. But Jesus' first thoughts, while speaking to Mary, are for those eleven men, his erring disciples. He calls them "brethren," the first time he ever called them that. It was a very loving term to show that he had not cast them off. All was pardoned, forgiven, and forgotten.

Mary departed on her joyful errand for Jesus, running. She had been surprised by joy, and now she could hardly wait to share the great "good news."

> That evening the disciples were meeting behind locked doors, in fear of the Jewish leaders, when suddenly Jesus was standing there among them! (John 20:19).

The hostility to Jesus that had put him on the cross was by no means dead. Now that word had gotten out that the tomb was empty, quite naturally this group of men did not know what was going to happen next. I think they felt like hunted men and frankly, I can't fault them for that. Word must have gotten around to each of them during the day, quite possibly carried by Mary Magdalene, telling the disciples that there would be a meeting that evening.

They were talking about him, with conflicting emotions of wonder, hope, and fear. Suddenly, in their midst, was the Presence. The door hadn't been opened; yet, he was there.

> He said to them, "Peace *be* with you." And when He had said this, He showed them both his hands and his side. The disciples therefore rejoiced when they saw the Lord.
> Jesus therefore said to them again, "Peace *be* with you; as the Father has sent me, I also send you" (vss. 19b-21 NAS).

Jesus stood in their midst, beyond the agony, beyond the tragedy, beyond the darkness that had so filled their hearts with terror. His first words to them were words of *peace.* "Peace," and not *blame.* "Peace," said a second time, and not *rebuke.* It was totally in keeping with the caring nature of

Christ. It was a word meant to calm and soothe their minds and wondering hearts.

As if sensing the question in their minds (Am I seeing an apparition?), Jesus supplied tangible evidence to convince them of the truth of his resurrection. The marks of the wounds remained on his body after the resurrection that they might be demonstrations of the truth of it. After a great victory, it is pointed out, the scars of a conqueror are marks of honor. (John, writing in the book of Revelation, tells us that even in the glory of heaven, Jesus appeared as a "Lamb that had been slain" [Rev. 5:6].) Jesus appeals to the senses of the disciples so that they would know for sure that he was not a phantom. There had been a bodily resurrection! Look and see, he was saying, I am your living Lord.

The effect was one of gladness and rejoicing on the part of the disciples. It revived their hearts; it wiped the tears from their eyes.

Jesus immediately brought the disciples back to the place where there was a recognition of responsibility. He entrusted them with a tremendous commission. To qualify them for their great mission, he gave them the gift of the Holy Spirit (vs. 22). Resources would be at their disposal that they had never had before and they would be equal to the work set before them in that Power.

THE ABSENT DISCIPLE AND HIS DOUBTS

One of the disciples, Thomas, "The Twin," was not there at the time with the others. When they kept telling him, "We have seen the Lord," he replied, "I won't believe it unless I see the nail wounds in his hands—and put my fingers into them—and place my hand into his side" (vss. 24, 25).

It was a crisis time in the lives of the eleven disciples, and Thomas should have been with them on that first resurrection evening. By his absence Thomas missed a great blessing. (When you absent yourself from fellowship with other believers, do you realize how much of blessing *you* miss?)

When the disciples saw Thomas, they enthusiastically told him, "We have seen the Lord!" Ten faithful men—men Thomas had come to know as being trustworthy and reliable —testified to this amazing fact, and yet he refused to take their word for it. He wanted incontestable evidence, personally experienced (his finger, the Lord's wounds).

Thomas was a good man. But a man with a very gloomy and doubting mind. I think it is fair to say that his despondency and moods kept him from really enjoying his religion. Thomas and his present-day successors only succeed in bringing heartache and trouble upon themselves. By being absent, and then refusing to believe, Thomas kept himself in suspense and unbelief for a whole week. It was doubtless a very melancholy week for Thomas, and he had no one to blame but himself.

JESUS APPEARS TO THE ELEVEN DISCIPLES

Christ deferred his next appearance to the disciples for another seven-night week. It was his purpose to gradually wean the disciples from his bodily presence. But it is also felt that by coming to them when he did the second time, he was showing that in the kingdom of the risen Messiah the first day of the week should be the day for rest and religious observance.

> Eight days later the disciples were together again, and this time Thomas was with them. The doors were locked; but suddenly, as before, Jesus was standing among them and greeting them. Then he said to Thomas, "Put your finger into my side. Don't be faithless any longer. Believe!"
> "My Lord and my God!" Thomas said.
> Then Jesus told him, "You believe because you have seen me. But blessed are those who haven't seen me and believe anyway" (vss. 26–29).

The circumstances were identical to those of the previous week—locked doors, sudden Presence, same words of greeting, "Peace *be* with you" (vs. 26b NAS).

Christ's Example Should Be Our Example

Jesus doesn't rebuke Thomas but tenderly cares for this weak member as he takes measures to heal and restore him. What Christ did for Thomas, we ought to be ready to do for others.

Jesus had regard for Thomas's faith, albeit it was in small measure. Thomas stood in his own light—dark pessimism—and missed seeing the Light of the world on that first resurrection evening. But now, suddenly, the room is once again illumined by the Presence of that Light, and Jesus is giving Thomas another opportunity. Jesus was fair to him because he loved Thomas. Jesus will be fair to you—you who may be so much like Thomas in thinking you have to see before you can believe, you who think you can trust only your senses. Jesus calls for Thomas's inquisitive forefinger and then his hand. Investigate, if you must, Thomas. (Use every faculty of your mind, dear friend, in your search for truth, but notice Jesus' final words to Thomas, because he is talking about you—if you can find it in your heart to believe where *you* cannot see, nor fully comprehend.)

Faith Comes Off Conqueror

Seeing sufficed. Unbelief struggled, but faith came off as conqueror. Thomas didn't have to touch Jesus to believe. The moment Thomas consented to belief, Jesus laid down a principle, the truth of which Christians of all ages have not been able to get away from. *Faith is believing where we cannot see.*

> "Thomas, because thou hast seen me, thou hast believed: blessed are they that have not seen, and yet have believed" (vs. 29 AV).

J. Wallace Hamilton asks the question, *If a man does not believe, is he to blame?* and answers it by pointing to Thomas. A man is at fault in his unbelief when, like Thomas, *he stands in his own light;* when *he won't come where the light is;* or when *he won't expose his mind to the light.*" [1] (Italics Hamilton's.)

Hamilton calls it trusting Christ beyond the horizon, much as we watch a ship sail out to sea, and off there on what we call the horizon, it disappears—it's gone. The horizon isn't real; it's only the limit of our vision, the place beyond which our sight cannot go. If we could only see a little farther, we would know the truth, that the ship is just as big and just as real as when it left the harbor. So it is with faith. Trusting God's Word (the Bible, and his revealed Word, Jesus) against the optic nerve!

The Jews had all the signs in the world—Jesus' miracles and his visible Presence—yet they did not believe. They crucified him! You cannot trust your senses. The Apostle Paul said, "The things which are seen are temporal; but the things which are not seen are eternal" (2 Cor. 4:18). That is fact, not just theology.

The choice is up to us: take that which is brief and fleeting, that which can be seen, or choose that which is deathless and eternal, lasting from everlasting to everlasting.

THE STATED PURPOSE OF JOHN'S GOSPEL

A towering testimony to the person of Christ—in the Presence of the Living Lord—prepared the way for John's summary statement, like an historian, arriving at a conclusion:

> Jesus' disciples saw him do many other miracles besides the ones told about in this book, but these are recorded so that you will believe that he is the Messiah, the Son of God, and that believing in him you will have life (vss. 30, 31).

John's design in writing was to bring men to Christ and ultimately to Heaven, and to persuade readers to believe so

[1] J. Wallace Hamilton, *What About Tomorrow* (Old Tappan, N.J.: Fleming H. Revell Co., 1972), p. 57.

that they would have the assurance of eternal life. Christ is to be the object of our faith.

The last great beatitude that our Lord uttered was to confirm our faith. Read what I have written, John says, and learn of the Messiah, Christ. And then, choose the way of faith, which will lead to eternal life with him where your faith will be rewarded by sight.

30

Call to Discipleship:
Love Triumphant

The Text: John 21
The Place: The Sea of Tiberias, also Called the Sea of
Galilee
The Event: Jesus' Seventh Post-Resurrection Appearance

It has been suggested that Christ's earthly ministry opened
with a party (the wedding in Cana of Galilee) and closed
with a picnic. Life for him was certainly not all parties
and picnics; but the thought is a happy one—Jesus concluding his earthly visitation in pleasant fellowship with his disciples with breakfast at the seashore!

> Later Jesus appeared again to the disciples beside the Lake
> of Galilee. This is how it happened:
> A group of us were there—Simon Peter, Thomas, "The
> Twin," Nathanael from Cana in Galilee, my brother James
> and I and two other disciples. Simon Peter said, "I'm going
> fishing." "We'll come too," we all said. We did, but caught
> nothing all night (John 21:1–3).

It is believed that the disciples had gone to Galilee while
waiting to return later to Jerusalem as Jesus had told them
they must do. What should they do in the interval? When
Jesus first called them to be his followers, they were fishermen.
These were not rich men and now, in order to meet their

temporal needs, I find it easy to believe they decided to use the time wisely in their profession—fishing.

Isn't it amazing that these humble fishermen, toiling all night in a boat, dragging about a cold, heavy, wet, empty net—men who found it necessary to work hard by the sweat of their brow in order that they and their families might eat and earn a living—these very men were the ones who went forth from an obscure corner of the globe, and literally turned the world upside down for Christ! That is tremendous!

Jesus evidently had a deep purpose and meaning in coming to his disciples at this Sea of Galilee (or Tiberias). Who will deny the influence of scenery and certain places in our thinking? We often link many memorable events with places. These well-known waters had been the scene of some of the most important events in the life of Christ and his followers.

HISTORY WAS REPEATING ITSELF

The disciples approached the gray dawn of early morning a tired, discouraged group of men. They had caught nothing. Contemporary fishermen know the feeling.

A STRANGER ON SHORE

At dawn we saw a man standing on the beach but couldn't see who he was. He called, "Any fish, boys?"

"No," we replied.

Then he said, "Throw out your net on the right-hand side of the boat, and you'll get plenty of them!" So we did, and couldn't draw in the net because of the weight of the fish, there were so many! (vss. 4–6).

THIS WASN'T JUST FISHERMEN'S LUCK

Then I said to Peter, "It is the Lord!" (vs. 7a). Jesus knew that they hadn't caught any fish, but this was his way to arrest their attention. John perceived the implications of what was happening. This was no stranger, and this wasn't just fishermen's luck! Jesus was performing another miracle on their behalf. Very lovingly, the Lord of glory addresses these men as "lads," or "boys."

JESUS IS INTERESTED IN THE COMMONPLACE AFFAIRS OF HIS PEOPLE

Jesus knew the disciples would be cold and hungry after a long night of unsuccessful toil. He is always interested in that which concerns his children—our physical needs are of great concern to the caring Jesus.

One word from John stating "It is the Lord," and Peter jumps overboard. His conduct is characteristic. He has been described as fervent, warm-hearted, impulsive, impetuous. affectionate, thinking nothing of consequences, acting on the spur of the moment, zealous, hasty, and enthusiastic. Exactly. That's Peter!

MAN OVERBOARD!

At that, Simon Peter put on his tunic (for he was stripped to the waist) and jumped into the water (and swam ashore). The rest of us stayed in the boat and pulled the loaded net to the beach, about 300 feet away (vss. 7, 8).

Peter couldn't wait to get to shore, no slow boat for him. If that was indeed Jesus, Peter couldn't make it to his side quick enough! (Peter forgot all about the net full of fish; in this he reminds me of the Samaritan woman who forgot her waterpot when Jesus revealed himself to her.)

BREAKFAST IS READY!

When we got there, we saw that a fire was kindled and fish were frying over it, and there was bread.

"Bring some of the fish you've just caught," Jesus said. So Simon Peter went out and dragged the net ashore. By his count there were 153 large fish; and yet the net hadn't torn (vss. 9–11).

They were wet and cold, weary and hungry. How good the frying fish smelled! John remembers vividly, "There was even bread!" Jesus has all the resources of heaven at his disposal to take care of the earthly needs of his people. Can you believe that? You can if you will see the deeper meaning behind this beautiful incident in Jesus' post-resurrection appearance. This is for *your* encouragement.

Jesus has called his followers to be fishers of men; and even though we get weary in our work, he is ever-present to supply our needs. Not always our wants, but definitely our needs. If there is one thing the resurrection is surely meant to show us, it is that it was not so much an event in history as a reality that has to be appropriated in our own everyday experiences. What the risen Christ offered when he showed himself alive, he holds out to us—the adequacy of himself.

The other disciples had to drag the net in. Matthew Henry says that if all the disciples had done as Peter did, what would have happened to the fish and the net? But he points out, if Peter hadn't done this, we wouldn't have this account of such holy zeal. Christ was pleased with both; both are needed— the zeal and enthusiasm that excites and motivates others, and the faithful, plodding worker.

There is one detail here that we must not overlook. It's Peter's obedience. Christ had said to bring some more fish, and instantly Peter moves into action. He doesn't wait for anyone else to do it. He not only makes up for the fact that he had previously abandoned his duty, but he leaves the side of Jesus to do his bidding. Peter even takes the time to count the fish. There were many more than they needed—153 is no small catch of fish. The fish could now be sold, and the money would help in the days ahead.

THE HOST SERVES

"Now come and have some breakfast!" Jesus said; and none of us dared ask him if he really was the Lord, for we were quite sure of it. Then Jesus went around serving us the bread and fish (vss. 12, 13).

How would you have felt to sit, eat, and drink in the Presence of someone who had just risen from the dead and could appear or disappear supernaturally. It was no small matter. Jesus was teaching the disciples that he would care for their bodies as well as their souls and spiritual well-being. He knows what it is to be fatigued, hungry, and discouraged. An old divine says, "Christ loveth to deal familiarly with men."

All of this they would think about, recalling it with pleasure and comfort in the difficult days ahead. John states:

> This was the third time Jesus had appeared to us since his return from the dead (vs. 14).

THE VALUE OF A PERSONAL RELATIONSHIP TO CHRIST

Jesus turns aside from serving his disciples and draws Peter into an unusual conversation. (Wouldn't it be great if all "after-meal" conversations among Christians would be as edifying as this!)

> After breakfast Jesus said to Simon Peter, "Simon, son of John, do you love me more than these others?"
>
> "Yes, Lord," Peter said, "you know I am your friend."
>
> "Then take care of my sheep," Jesus said.
>
> Once more he asked him, "Simon, son of John, are you even my friend?"
>
> Peter was grieved at the way Jesus asked the question this third time. "Lord, you know my heart; you know I am," he said.
>
> Jesus said, "Then feed my little sheep. When you were young, you were able to do as you liked and go wherever you wanted to; but when you are old, you will stretch out your hands and others will direct you and take you where you don't want to go."
>
> Jesus said this to let him know what kind of death he would die to glorify God. Then Jesus told him, "Follow me" (vss. 15–19).

How could Peter best forget that he had denied his Lord by the side of a fire built by Jesus' enemies? How wise our Lord is! Yes, Peter could best forget by now *confessing* him by the side of a fire built by Jesus himself! Three times Peter had denied our Lord! Now, three times Jesus gives him the opportunity to confess him!

While the denial was in the darkness of night, the confession would come in the dawning glow of a new day. The denial was the answer of cowardice to the hatred of Jesus' foes; the confession would be the answer of courage to the power of Love. But the confession went far beyond the denial. This Jesus proved by commissioning Peter for special service. To those who truly love him, even though they may have momentarily faltered and failed in some manner, Jesus will continue to show himself faithful and show his confidence in them for future service.

DIALOGUE FOR DECISION

The dialogue was meant to lead Peter along the path of decision. Jesus would launch him on a new era of work with the same words with which he was originally called: "Follow me." Peter's declaration of devoted love restores him to full service in the presence of the other disciples. Christ could not entrust the care of his "sheep" to anyone who did not love him and have a heart for him and his work. Peter, as under-shepherd, was to feed Christ's lambs, to tend his sheep, and to feed the sheep. We know how carefully Peter guarded this sacred trust.

Peter, later, in writing to the scattered Jewish Christians, gives a special word to the elders of the Church. He says: "Fellow elders, this is my plea to you: Feed the flock of God; care for it willingly, not grudgingly; not for what you will get out of it, but because you are eager to serve the Lord. Don't be tyrants, but lead them by your good example, and when the Head Shepherd comes, your reward will be a never-ending share in his glory and honor" (I Peter 5:1b–4).

Did Peter understand the dialogue with Jesus? Did Peter give the right answers and make the correct decision? The Cross and the risen Christ were the guiding force of his life. Peter would travel on with Jesus! That following, that traveling, Jesus now tells him, would lead to some painful experiences in his later life. The tradition of the ancients tells us that Peter was crucified at Rome under Nero, A.D. 68, or, as others say, 79. But it is certain, whatever the manner of death, Peter died a martyr's death even as Christ said in this decisive hour of conversing with Peter.

PETER WAS HUMAN

Peter's eyes look from Jesus to John, his familiar friend. Whether he was overly concerned about John's future (since Jesus had just told him what his would be), or what his motives were, I cannot say. He did a very human thing. Jesus sets him straight and thereby shows his authority over all his servants.

> Peter asked Jesus, "What about him, Lord? What sort of death will he die?"
> Jesus replied, "If I want him to live until I return, what is that to you? You follow me" (vss. 21b, 22).

It is not for us to inquire about another's place in the plans of Jesus. We are to show an interest, yes, but not to intrude. Jesus' answer shows that his will for one life may be quite different from his will for another. Tradition tells us that John died a natural death after a long and useful life.

THE CONCLUSION OF JOHN'S STORY

John's writing is a standing and eloquent testimony to Christ as being the Eternal Word sent from God. John closed as he began. Much more could have been written, but he is satisfied that what he has related is true, all true.

I saw these events and have recorded them here. And we all know that my account of these things is accurate. And I suppose that if all the other events in Jesus' life were written, the whole world could hardly contain the books! (vss. 24, 25).

Yes, John, what you have written is but a fraction of the whole (our indebtedness knows no measure). But this is the amazing thing—we can be a part of that continuing story of love triumphant, for we, too, have heard that call to discipleship. Jesus' concern for his disciples is the same concern he has for you and me. Let us make certain our response to the question he asked of Peter, "Do you *really* love me?," is one of unhesitating, unqualified surrender, a total yielding to the one who loved us so much, he died for us.